INSIDE YO... ANNUAL 2025!

INSIDE...

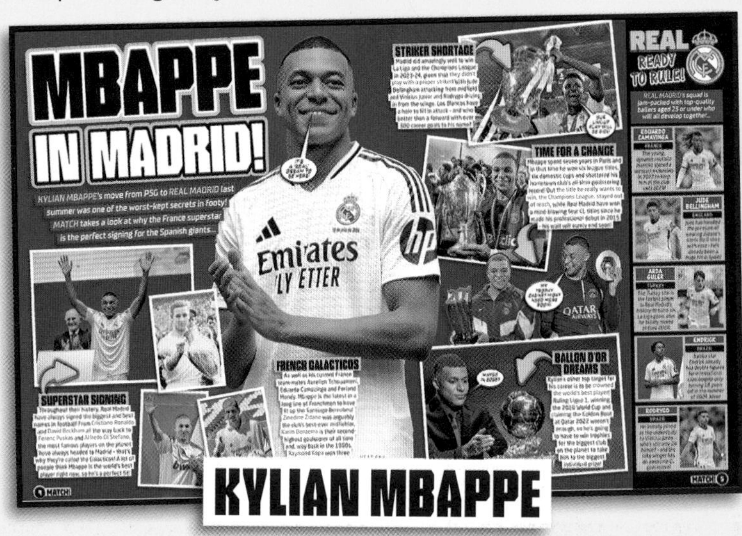

MBAPPE IN MADRID!

IT'S A 'REAL' DREAM TO BE HERE!

KYLIAN MBAPPE's move from PSG to REAL MADRID last summer was one of the worst-kept secrets in footy! MATCH takes a look at why the France superstar is the perfect signing for the Spanish giants...

SUPERSTAR SIGNING

Throughout their history, Real Madrid have always signed the biggest and best names in football! From Cristiano Ronaldo and David Beckham all the way back to Ferenc Puskas and Alfredo Di Stefano, the most famous players on the planet have always headed to Madrid – that's why they're called the Galacticos! A lot of people think Mbappe is the world's best player right now, so he's a perfect fit!

FRENCH GALACTICOS

As well as his current France team-mates Aurelien Tchouameni, Eduardo Camavinga and Ferland Mendy, Mbappe is the latest in a long line of Frenchmen to have lit up the Santiago Bernabeu! Zinedine Zidane was arguably the club's best-ever midfielder, Karim Benzema is their second-highest goalscorer of all time and, way back in the 1950s, Raymond Kopa won three European Cups with the club!

STRIKER SHORTAGE

Madrid did amazingly well to win La Liga and the Champions League in 2023-24, given that they didn't play with a proper striker! With Jude Bellingham attacking from midfield and Vinicius Junior and Rodrygo driving in from the wings, Los Blancos have a hole to fill in attack – and who better than a forward with over 300 career goals to his name?

TIME FOR A CHANGE

Mbappe spent seven years in Paris and in that time he won six league titles, six domestic cups and shattered his hometown club's all-time goalscoring record! But the title he really wants to win, the Champions League, stayed out of reach, while Real Madrid have won a mind-blowing four CL titles since he made his professional debut in 2015 – his wait will surely end soon!

BALLON D'OR DREAMS

Kylian's other top target for his career is to be crowned the world's best player! Ruling Ligue 1, winning the 2018 World Cup and claiming the Golden Boot at Qatar 2022 weren't enough, so he's going to have to win trophies for the biggest club on the planet to take him to the biggest individual prize!

REAL READY TO RULE!

REAL MADRID's squad is jam-packed with top-quality ballers aged 23 or under who will all develop together...

EDUARDO CAMAVINGA
FRANCE

The young, dynamic midfield maestro signed a contract extension in 2023 to keep him at the club until 2029!

JUDE BELLINGHAM
ENGLAND

Jude has handled the pressure of wearing Zidane's iconic No.5 shirt with ease – he's already been a huge hit in Spain!

ARDA GULER
TURKEY

The Turkey star is the fastest player in Real Madrid's history to score six La Liga goals, plus he totally rocked at Euro 2024!

ENDRICK
BRAZIL

Samba star Endrick already has double figures for international caps despite only turning 18 years old in the summer of 2024. Wow!

RODRYGO
BRAZIL

He initially joined as the understudy to Vinicius Junior – who's still only 24 himself – and the silky winger has an awesome CL goal record!

SOUTHGATE YOU'RE THE ONE!

After GARETH SOUTHGATE stepped down as ENGLAND manager last summer, MATCH looks back at some of his highlights...

SING IT LOUDER, I CAN'T HEAR YOU!

DAZZLING DEBUTANTS!

Having started out as England's Under-21 manager, Southgate was always going to give young players their chance! He handed Three Lions debuts to 66 players during his reign, including the likes of Jude Bellingham, Phil Foden, Bukayo Saka and Cole Palmer, while his most recent debutants were Jarrad Branthwaite and Adam Wharton!

It's ultra-rare for an England manager to get their own chant, but Southgate defo earned it after England's 2018 World Cup efforts! "Southgate, You're The One", to the tune of Atomic Kitten's 2000 hit "Whole Again", was blasted out by fans throughout his reign and went viral again after Three Lions supporters sang it to a lookalike German police officer during Euro 2024. LOL!

WORLD CUP WAISTCOAT!

Southgate set the fashion trend of the summer in 2018 with his waistcoat in Russia! Many people dubbed it a lucky charm after The Three Lions reached the semi-finals of the World Cup for the first time since 1990, including an epic penalty shootout victory over Colombia, only to be knocked out by Luka Modric's Croatia!

SOUTHGATE'S STATS!

GAMES	WINS	DRAWS	LOSSES	WIN %
102	61	24	17	59.8

SOUTHGATE SCRAPBOOK!

2016

Southgate is named England manager! He was promoted from the U21s after previously managing Middlesbrough!

2018

He leads England to their first World Cup semi-final for 28 years, before suffering defeat to Croatia. Gutted!

2018

The Three Lions win in Spain for the first time in 31 years en route to the UEFA Nations League Finals!

EPIC TOURNO RECORD!

Southgate won more matches at major tournaments (World Cups and European Championships) than any other England manager in history! They reached the final in two of his four major tournaments in charge – a feat they'd achieved just once (in 1966) at their previous 23 World Cup and Euro appearances before his reign began. Legend!

MEMORABLE MOMENTS!

During Southgate's reign, England gave fans some of their most memorable moments in history! The penalty shootout win over Colombia in 2018 was their first-ever World Cup shootout success, their Euro 2020 knockout victories v Germany and Denmark produced two of the best atmospheres ever at Wembley, and Jude Bellingham's overhead-kick v Slovakia and Ollie Watkins' 90th-minute winner v Netherlands last summer were pure limbs!

As well as Toni Kroos and Thiago Alcantara retiring from football altogether, these legends left the international game in 2024!

Thomas Muller

Germany's third most capped player stepped down and was later joined by Manuel Neuer!

Jan Vertonghen

Belgium's most capped player ever racked up 157 appearances for The Red Devils. Wow!

Olivier Giroud

France's all-time top goalscorer was part of their epic 2018 World Cup-winning squad. Hero!

Xherdan Shaqiri

Switzerland's second most capped player was followed by legendary GK Yann Sommer!

Angel Di Maria

Argentina's joint-third most capped player called time on national duty after the 2024 Copa America!

England reach their first final for 55 years at the delayed Euro 2020 after a dramatic knockout-round run!

Southgate signs a second contract extension that would keep him in charge until December 2024!

England beat Wales 3-0 in the Battle of Britain to qualify for the knockout rounds of the 2022 World Cup!

England reach the final of Euro 2024 thanks to a late goal from super sub Ollie Watkins v Netherlands!

Southgate resigns as England manager after their Euro 2024 Final defeat to Spain! Thanks for the memories, Gareth!

THE NEW-LOOK

CLUB WORLD

2025 is a huge year for world football, as the first edition of the new-look Club World Cup kicks off! The competition has divided opinion though, so what's it all about? MATCH takes a look...

WHAT'S WRONG WITH THE OLD FORMAT?

The tournament used to involve seven teams and be played every December, but it didn't create much excitement. It was played at an awkward time in the season and Europe totally dominated – in 2023, Man. City became the 11th European team in a row to lift the trophy after beating South American champions Fluminense in the final!

WHO'S PLAYING?

We won't know the full line-up until the end of 2024, but 29 teams have already booked in...

EUROPE	
CHELSEA	England
REAL MADRID	Spain
MAN. CITY	England
BAYERN MUNICH	Germany
PSG	France
INTER	Italy
PORTO	Portugal
BENFICA	Portugal
BORUSSIA DORTMUND	Germany
JUVENTUS	Italy
ATLETICO MADRID	Spain
RED BULL SALZBURG	Austria

SOUTH AMERICA	
PALMEIRAS	Brazil
FLAMENGO	Brazil
FLUMINENSE	Brazil
RIVER PLATE	Argentina

CONCACAF	
MONTERREY	Mexico
SEATTLE SOUNDERS	USA
LEON	Mexico
PACHUCA	Mexico

AFRICA	
AL AHLY	Egypt
WYDAD CASABLANCA	Morocco
ESPERANCE	Tunisia
MAMELODI SUNDOWNS	S. Africa

ASIA	
AL HILAL	Saudi Arabia
URAWA RED DIAMONDS	Japan
AL AIN	United Arab Emirates
ULSAN HD	South Korea

OCEANIA	
AUCKLAND CITY	New Zealand

FACTPACK

WHAT? *The 2025 FIFA Club World Cup*

WHEN? *June 15-July 13* **WHERE?** *USA*

WHO? *Next summer, teams from all over the world will head to the USA to compete in the FIFA Club World Cup. It's not a brand new tournament, but it is a new format – now, 32 teams will be involved, with a group stage and knockout rounds just like the international World Cup!*

HOW ARE THE TEAMS CHOSEN?

Africa, Asia and North & Central America (CONCACAF) get four spots at the tournament each, with one from Oceania, six from South America and 12 from Europe. The places were given to all the continental champions over the last four years, plus the best-performing teams in each continent's top club competition in that time!

TUNNEL VISION!

Check out some of the best tunnels from around the world!

ARENA AUFSCHALKE GERMANY

UEFA EURO2024 GERMANY

Schalke updated their tunnel to look like a mineshaft!

CALIENTE STADIUM MEXICO

We love the Aztec design at Club Tijuana's ground!

CUP!

WHO ELSE WILL PLAY?

We'll know the two other South American teams after the Copa Libertadores final in November 2024. As hosts, the US will get another spot as well, so the last team will come from MLS!

WHY NOW?

The World Cup is the biggest tournament in the world, but it only happens every four years so FIFA created another massive competition for club teams! They want to see teams from all over the planet battling with Europe's giants to be crowned the best team in the world! Also, for the USA, it'll be a warm-up for 2026 World Cup when they'll host the FIFA World Cup!

WHAT'S THE PROBLEM?

Some people think that there are already too many games, so another tournament in the middle of the summer is not ideal! When the competition kicks off in June 2025, European teams should be resting to prepare for the new season, so they might not send their first-team players to the US!

FIFA CLUB WORLD CUP

TOP TEN WOMEN'S TRANSFERS

Check out the most expensive female footballers of all time!

#	Player	Transfer	Fee
1	RACHEAL KUNDANANJI	Madrid CFF to Bay FC	£685,000
2	BARBRA BANDA	Shanghai Shengli to Orlando Pride	£582,000
3	MAYRA RAMIREZ	Levante to Chelsea	£426,000
4	KEIRA WALSH	Man. City to Barcelona	£400,000
5	TARCIANE	Corinthians to Houston Dash	£390,000
6	LENA OBERDORF	Wolfsburg to Bayern Munich	£384,000
7	KIKA NAZARETH	Benfica to Barcelona	£339,000
8	EWA PAJOR	Wolfsburg to Barcelona	£338,000
9	KYRA COONEY-CROSS	Hammarby to Arsenal	£301,000
10	JILL ROORD	Wolfsburg to Man. City	£300,000

Transfers correct up to July 2024.

RAJKO MITIC STADIUM SERBIA

Red Star Belgrade's stadium is terrifying for visitors!

JUAN CARMELO ZERILLO STADIUM ARGENTINA

Gimnasia players enter the pitch via a dog's mouth!

ANFIELD ENGLAND

Liverpool have one of football's most famous tunnels!

TOP TEN BRITS ABROAD

CL FINAL SPECIAL!

MATCH has dived into the history books to reveal the British players to start a Champions League final for a non-British club...

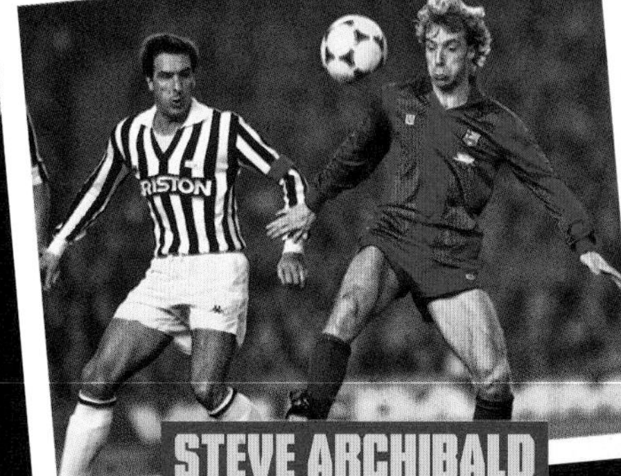

STEVE ARCHIBALD

BARCELONA ★ 1986

Scotland striker Archibald had three good seasons in Barcelona after leaving Tottenham in 1984, scoring more than 30 goals and winning La Liga in his first campaign! Unfortunately for him though, he was also on the end of one of the biggest shocks in European Cup history, as Barca lost on penalties to Romanian underdogs Steaua Bucharest in the 1986 final!

LAURIE CUNNINGHAM

REAL MADRID ★ 1981

Cunningham was the first British player to play for Real Madrid, joining the Spanish giants in 1979 after dazzling for West Brom. A wicked winger known for tearing full-backs to shreds, he helped them reach the 1981 European Cup final, where they lost 1-0 to Liverpool – Los Blancos haven't lost a CL final since!

KEVIN KEEGAN

HAMBURG ★ 1980

In the late 1970s, Keegan was the biggest name in English footy. As well as winning three league titles and a European Cup with Liverpool, plus the Bundesliga crown with Hamburg, he'd also won two Ballons d'Or! He suffered heartbreak in his third season in Germany though, as the club reached their first European Cup final but lost 1-0 to Nottingham Forest!

JUDE BELLINGHAM

REAL MADRID ★ 2024

What a debut season Bellingham had in Spain! After firing Real Madrid to La Liga glory with 19 goals, he then rocked up in his home country's national stadium and picked up the Champions League trophy against his former club – all before his 21st birthday! The former Dortmund man wasn't at his best, but set up Vinicius Junior for Real's crucial second goal!

SEEING DOUBLE!

If you thought taking on one Kylian Mbappe was hard enough, imagine facing two of the Real Madrid and France star! World-famous waxworks company Madame Tussauds created this incredibly lifelike creation for KM!

UNFAMILIAR FEELING!

Bayer Leverkusen's invincible title-winning triumph of 2023-24 ended one of the most impressive records in football...Kingsley Coman's 11-season run of winning a league title with Bayern Munich, Juventus and PSG! It was his first senior campaign without a league winners' medal!

BROMLEY BOUNCE!

By winning the National League play-off final on penalties against Solihull Moors, Bromley entered the English Football League for the first time in their 132-year history, becoming the 147th club to join the EFL fold!

CHRIS WADDLE

MARSEILLE ★ 1991

Poor old Waddle. In 1990, he fired over the crossbar in England's World Cup semi-final shootout defeat to Germany, then a year later lost another huge game on penalties - the 1991 European Cup final! A left-footed winger with tons of tricks, Waddle was Marseille's main man on the road to the final, but couldn't find a way past Red Star Belgrade!

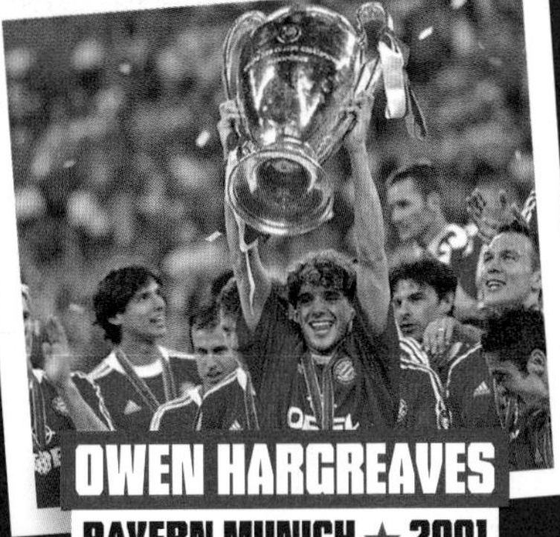

OWEN HARGREAVES

BAYERN MUNICH ★ 2001

Jadon Sancho is one of many young Brits to have joined a European academy in recent years, but back in the 1990s it was far less common. Born in Canada to English parents, Hargreaves joined Bayern's youth ranks at 16 and played all 120 minutes of their 2001 CL final with Valencia, which they won on penalties!

PAUL LAMBERT

BORUSSIA DORTMUND ★ 1997

If you love your footy legends, then you'll know all about France playmaker Zinedine Zidane. In 1997, he inspired Juventus all the way to the CL final, but barely got a kick on the night because of one man - Lambert! Not only did the Scotland defensive midfielder produce an inch-perfect man-marking job on Zizou in Dortmund's 3-1 win, he also set up their first goal in the final!

GARETH BALE

REAL MADRID ★ 2014, 2016, 2017 & 2018

Bale is the most successful British player in CL history! Every final he played in was special - in 2014 he notched a crucial goal in extra-time, in 2016 he was Real's driving attacking force and bagged in the penalty shootout, in 2017 he lifted the trophy in his home city of Cardiff and in 2018 he scored one of the best goals in CL final history with a stunning overhead kick!

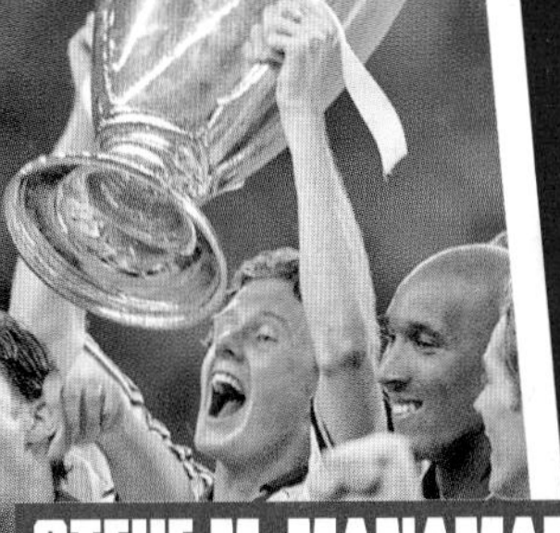

STEVE McMANAMAN

REAL MADRID ★ 2000 & 2002

These days you might know "Macca" as a CL commentator, but he used to be a star on the pitch on European nights! The winger left Liverpool for Real Madrid in 1999 and lifted the big trophy in his first season, scoring a brilliant volley against Valencia in the final! Two years later, he was a champion again, coming off the bench in the final against Bayer Leverkusen!

JADON SANCHO

BORUSSIA DORTMUND ★ 2024

Sancho struggled to make an impact after joining Manchester United in 2021, but he found his form after going back to Dortmund in January. He was one of the stars of the semi-final as they dumped out PSG, but couldn't unlock Real's defence at Wembley before being replaced late on by another exciting young English talent - wicked winger Jamie Bynoe-Gittens!

WOMEN'S CHAMPIONS LEAGUE

Four British women have started in CL finals for non-British clubs, too...

JESS FISHLOCK

LYON ★ 2019

Fishlock got a CL medal with FFC Frankfurt in 2015, but left before they won the final. The Wales legend made up for it four years later though, starting in Lyon's 4-1 win over Barcelona!

TONI DUGGAN

BARCELONA ★ 2019

The ex-Man. City and Everton striker was one of the WSL's all-time leading scorers when she joined Barcelona in 2017, and scored five times on the road to the 2018-19 Champions League final!

KEIRA WALSH

BARCELONA ★ 2023 & 2024

Barca have a special player in midfield in the form of Spain World Cup winner Aitana Bonmati, but Walsh slotted in alongside her for the 2023 and 2024 CL finals like she'd been a team-mate her whole life!

LUCY BRONZE

LYON ★ 2018, 2019 & 2020
BARCELONA ★ 2023 & 2024

Lyon and Barcelona are arguably the two best women's club sides of all-time - and Bronze has played for both of them! In May 2024, she picked up her fifth CL winners' medal!

REMEMBER THE NAME...

The 17-year-old Tottenham sensation became the club's youngest-ever Premier League player in 2024 and apparently turned down interest from Real Madrid and PSG to sign his first pro contract with the club!

BRANTHWAITE'S WHEELS!

England centre-back Jarrad Branthwaite told MATCH that his best Christmas present was an Audi R8 driving experience when he was 14 years old. Lucky guy!

WSL LEGEND!

In 2024, Aston Villa midfielder Jordan Nobbs maintained her record of being the only player to score in all 14 seasons of the Women's Super League, including the 2017 Spring Series. Class!

WIN PRIZES!

RIG 300 PRO COSMIC PURPLE GAMING HEADSET!

Thanks to our mates at NACON, you could win this wicked RIG 300 PRO Cosmic Purple Gaming Headset for PlayStation! We've got nine of the top-quality headsets up for grabs. Get in there!

HOW TO ENTER! VISIT...SHOP.KELSEY.CO.UK/WIN

Then click on the competition image and enter your details. Full T&Cs are available online.

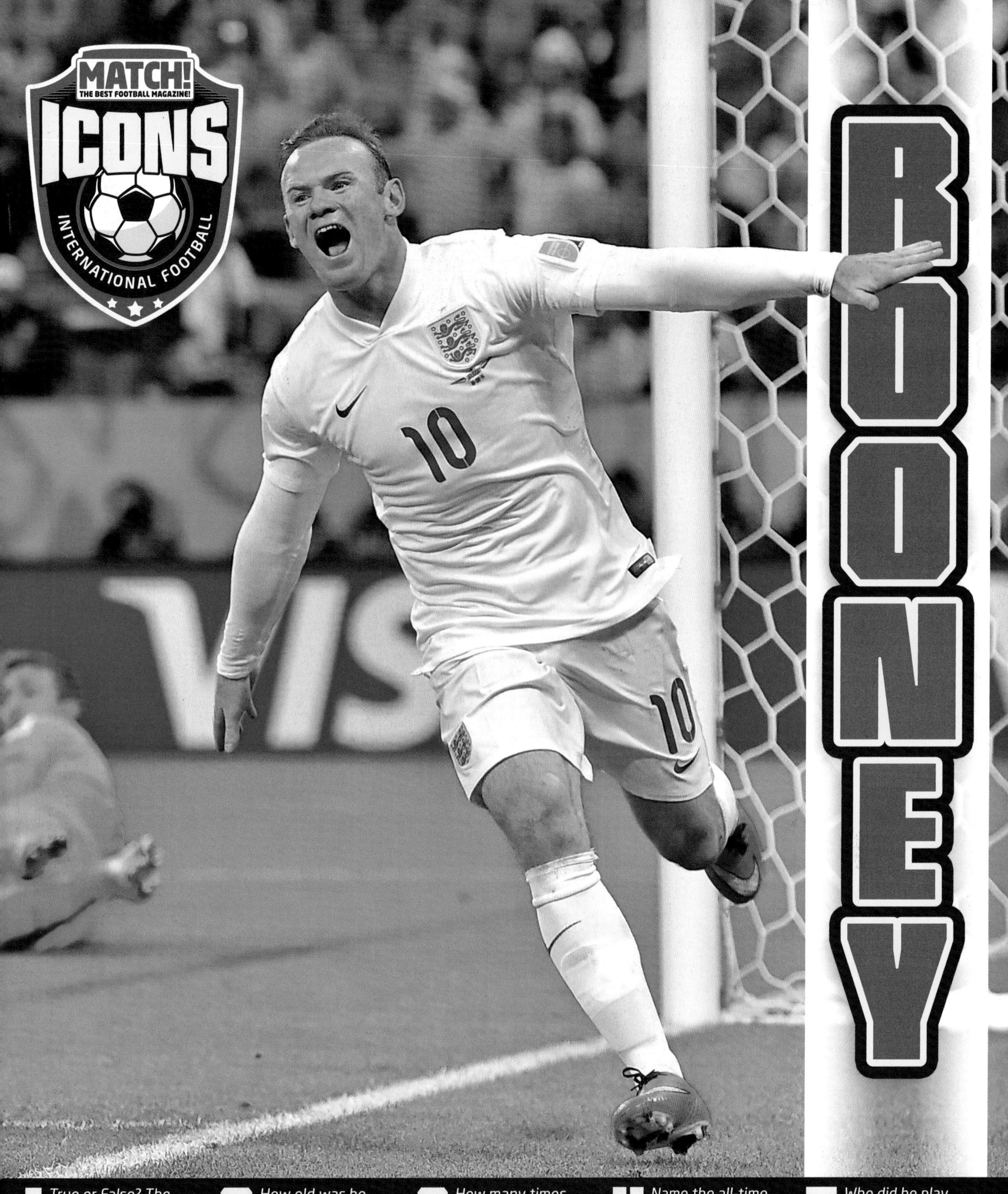

1 True or False? The Three Lions legend could have chosen to represent Republic of Ireland instead of England!

2 How old was he when he became England's youngest-ever goalscorer - 15, 16, 17 or 18 years old?

3 How many times was Rooney named England's senior Player of the Year - twice, three times or four times?

4 Name the all-time legend that Wazza overtook to become The Three Lions' record goalscorer in 2015!

5 Who did he play his final England game against in 2018 - Australia, Canada, Argentina or USA?

ANSWERS ON PAGE 94

ULTIMATE GUIDE TO... WOMEN'S EURO 2025

MATCH picks out the big storylines to keep an eye out for in the 2025 Women's European Championship!

1 THE HOSTS

Euro 2025 will be the first major tournament in Switzerland since they co-hosted the men's Euros with Austria in 2008! The Swiss saw off competition from France, Poland and a joint Scandinavian bid from Denmark, Finland, Norway and Sweden for the right to host – turn over to see the grounds they'll use!

2 FANTASTIC FANS

Switzerland are expecting over 720,000 supporters to turn up and fill the stadiums over the four weeks of the tournament! Not only would that make it the biggest sporting event in the country's history, it'll also be nearly 150,000 more spectators than that attended in 2022 – the Women's Euros just keep getting bigger and better!

3 THE HOLDERS

England were deserved winners of the European crown in 2022, bossing their way to the final and a first-ever major international trophy! Retaining the title away from home will be an even bigger challenge, but Sarina Wiegman's team have the quality and belief to do it!

4 QUALIFYING

The qualifying rounds used the same format as the UEFA Nations League, with four-team groups in three leagues. The top two countries in the League A groups – Spain, Germany, France, Italy, Iceland, Denmark, England and the Netherlands – have all secured their spots already, with seven other places decided via play-offs in October 2024!

5 THE FAVOURITES

The Lionesses might be the holders, but world champions Spain will be the team to beat. They've hardly lost a match since beating England in the 2023 World Cup final, have added a UEFA Nations League to their trophy cabinet, and their squad is packed with Barcelona's Champions League winners! Can anyone stop them?

6

GOLDEN GIRL'S REVENGE

In 2022, defensive midfielder Lena Oberdorf was named the inaugural Young Player of the Tournament as Germany finished runners-up. It was little consolation – as witnessed by her tears when she collected the award at Wembley – so she'll be desperate to help her country go one better this time around!

7

THE DRAW

Get the date December 16, 2024 locked into your diary – that's when the groups will be drawn for the final tournament and we'll find out who's playing who! The tournament kicks off on July 2, with the final also in Basel on July 27!

8

BONMATI THE BEST

Of all the Spanish stars, Aitana Bonmati shines brightest. The Barca midfielder can control games totally on her own – that's why she won the FIFA Best and Ballon d'Or awards in 2023, and she'll hold on to those crowns if she dominates again in Switzerland!

9

BATTLE FOR THE GOLDEN BOOT

Last time, England's Beth Mead and Alexandra Popp of Germany topped the scoring charts with six goals each – but the lethal Lioness took the Golden Boot with five assists! Both players will be hunting the prize again, along with stars like Salma Paralluelo of Spain and France forward Marie-Antoinette Katoto!

10

FINALISSIMA

Whoever wins the Euros will get the chance to add another trophy to their collection, by taking on the South American champions in the Finalissima! The date of the clash is still to be decided, but England are the holders after they beat Brazil on penalties in the first edition in 2023!

WOMEN'S EURO 2025...

STADIUM GUIDE!

MATCH reveals the awesome stadiums that'll be used in Switzerland...

ST. JAKOB-PARK

City: Basel ★ **Capacity:** 38,512

The Women's Euros finals begins and ends here, in Switzerland's biggest football stadium! It's seen plenty of big Champions League nights as well as lots of international football, so it's the perfect venue for the final!

STADION WANKDORF

City: Bern ★ **Capacity:** 31,783

Bern's original stadium hosted the 1954 men's World Cup final, but that was knocked down in 2001 to make room for this modern ground. It's the home to Switzerland's No.1 men's side, BSC Young Boys!

STADE DE GENEVE

City: Geneva ★ **Capacity:** 30,084

Along with Basel, Bern and Zurich, Geneva's stadium hosted games at the men's Euros in 2008. Switzerland were dumped out in the group stage then - the women's team will be hoping for better luck!

KYBUNPARK

City: St. Gallen ★ **Capacity:** 19,694

Kybunpark is one of the newest grounds that will be used at these finals (built in 2008), but it's home to the oldest club in Switzerland, St. Gallen (founded in 1879)! It's next to a huge shopping centre!

SWISSPORARENA

City: Luzern ★ **Capacity:** 16,800

Fans of Hibernian might recognise the Swissporarena - it was here that their team knocked out Swiss side Luzern in the qualifying rounds of the 2023-24 Europa Conference League!

STADE DE TOURBILLON

City: Sion ★ **Capacity:** 16,263

Originally built in 1968, and renovated in 1989, this will be the oldest stadium at Euro 2025. It takes its name from the Tourbillon Castle, which sits on top of a mountain overlooking the city of Sion!

LETZIGRUND

City: Zurich ★ **Capacity:** 26,104

This ground, which will host one of the semi-finals, is home to both of the city's men's teams - Zurich and Grasshoppers, who have one of the biggest derbies in Switzerland! It's no stranger to big matches!

STOCKHORN ARENA

City: Thun ★ **Capacity:** 10,398

It might be the smallest stadium at these finals but, sat on the shores of Lake Thun with the Swiss Alps looming high above, the Stockhorn Arena probably has the best views! Fans will love it!

WOMEN'S EURO RECORDS!

MATCH dives into the footy record books to tell you everything you need to know about the history of the Women's Euros! Check this all out...

EURO QUEENS

With eight trophies to their name, Germany are the undisputed queens of the Women's Euros! They were especially dominant between 1995 and 2013, winning six tournaments in a row and going 26 games unbeaten! With a run like that, it's no surprise that they've also won more matches (36) and scored more goals (107) than any other team in the competition's history!

LEGENDARY LIONESSES

England set new standards when they won the trophy in 2022. Sarina Wiegman's team were especially dominant in the group stage, scoring a record 14 goals thanks to a totally dominant 8-0 win against Norway – the biggest win in the competition's history! On the way to the trophy, they became only the third team to win six games in one tournament, ended with a record 22 goals, then, to top if all off, they brought a record 87,192 crowd to the final at Wembley!

GOLDEN BOOT

Every striker in Switzerland will be eyeing the Golden Boot! Nobody's ever scored more than six goals at a Women's Euros, with three players - Inka Grings for Germany in 2009, England's Beth Mead and Germany's Alexandra Popp in 2022 - hitting the tally. Popp deserves a special shout out though for being the first player to score in five Women's Euro games in a row!

BIRGIT PRINZ-ESS

Germany legend Birgit Prinz has so many Women's Euros records it's hard to believe! As well as winning a joint-record five championships, she's also the tournament's joint-record goalscorer with ten, plus she's played 23 matches at the finals - more than any other player! But the craziest stat might be the fact that she became the youngest goalscorer in a final after netting against Sweden at the age of 17 in 1995, then 14 years later bagged again against England to become the oldest player to score in a final too!

UNLUCKY LOSERS

As the only team to make it to two finals without lifting the trophy, Italy have one of the Women's Euros' most unwanted records! They've also suffered the most losses and conceded the most goals, but at least they've got a couple of silver medals to show for their efforts - France have played at seven WEuros without ever getting further than the semis - and that was just once in 2022!

13 *Editions of the Women's Euros that have taken place before 2025 - Switzerland will be number 14!*

1984 *The year of the first-ever Women's Euros, when only four teams were involved!*

2017 *Year that the competition was expanded to 16 nations for the first time!*

12 *Tournaments that Italy and Norway have qualified for - more than any other team!*

5 *Countries that have got their hands on the trophy in its history - Germany, Norway, Sweden, Netherlands and England!*

18 *Minutes that it took for Sweden forward Lena Videkull to score three goals against Norway in 1995 - the fastest ever WEuros hat-trick!*

0 *Goals that Norway conceded en route to the trophy back in 1993 - the only team ever to keep a clean sheet in every game, although they did only play two matches!*

49 *Seconds that it took for striker Linda Sallstrom to score for Finland against Spain at Euro 2022 - the fastest goal in the tournament's history!*

95 *Goals scored by all teams combined at the 2022 Euros finals - a new tournament record!*

16 *Years and 351 days - the age of Norway striker Isabell Herlovsen when she became the youngest goalscorer in Women's Euros history back in 2005!*

8 *Goals scored in the 2009 Women's Euros final, when Germany thumped England 6-2!*

WOMEN'S EUROS...

BOARD GAME!

GAME RULES!

Find a mate or family member to take on, grab a dice and use a counter or coin to keep track of your progress on the board!

Follow the instructions as you move on every square, and keep a tally of each player's goals for and against!

If you receive two yellow cards or a red card, get injured or substituted, go right back to square one!

The winner is the player that reaches the end of the final with the best goal difference! What are you waiting for?

KICK-OFF! ➡ 1 MIN
Let's get the Women's Euros final started!
ROLL A SIX TO START!

ACTION! ➡ 3 MINS
You're in on goal, but the defender tracks back to tackle you!

GOAL CHANCE! ➡ 5 MINS
You're through one-on-one!
ROLL EVENS TO SCORE, ROLL ODD FOR THE KEEPER TO SAVE IT!

INJURY? ⬇ 10 MINS
Your marker crashes into you!
ROLL EVENS TO GET BACK UP, ROLL ODD FOR A CALF INJURY!

⬅ GOAL? 11 MINS
The opposition break forward!
ROLL EVENS TO STOP THEM, ODD MEANS THEY SCORE!

⬅ ACTION! 14 MINS
Your team-mate breaks forward from midfield and you put them through!

⬅ GOAL CHANCE! 15 MINS
You hit a 30-yard screamer!
ROLL EVENS AND IT RIPS THE NET, ROLL ODD AND IT'S SAVED!
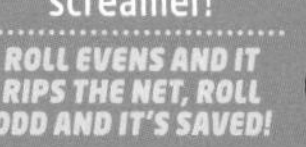

⬅ ACTION! 17 MINS
You make a raiding run down the wing, but get tackled and win a throw-in!

⬅ YELLOW CARD? 19 MINS
You tug your opponent's shirt!
EVENS GETS A WARNING, ROLL ODD FOR A BOOKING!

⬇ INJURY? 22 MINS
You jump for the ball!
EVENS WINS THE HEADER, ROLL ODD TO CLASH HEADS!

ACTION! ➡ 24 MINS
You get closed down quickly, but bust out a jaw-dropping trick. Legend!

RED CARD? ➡ 26 MINS
You're defending on your own line!
EVENS CLEARS THE BALL, ODD AND YOU SEE RED FOR HANDBALL!

GOAL CHANCE! ➡ 28 MINS
You meet a corner with a header!
ROLL EVENS AND YOU SCORE, ROLL ODD AND YOU HEAD IT OVER!

ACTION! ➡ 31 MINS
You launch a pinpoint cross-field pass to your full-back!

ACTION! ➡ 34 MINS
You follow up a rebound, but their goalkeeper makes a wicked save. Gutted!

GOAL? ⬇ 36 MINS
You give away a free-kick!
EVENS AND IT'S BLOCKED, ODD AND IT'S A GOAL!

⬅ GOAL CHANCE! 37 MINS
You power a header at goal!
ROLL EVENS TO NOD HOME, ROLL ODD TO HIT THE BAR!

⬅ ACTION! 40 MINS
You dummy the ball and completely fool your opponent!

⬅ OFFSIDE! 42 MINS
Your team-mate makes a run, but you delay the pass too long!

⬅ HALF-TIME! 45 MINS
Get a drink before starting the second half!

⬅ KICK-OFF! 46 MINS
The second half begins!

⬇ GOAL CHANCE! 49 MINS
You win a penalty!
ROLL EVENS AND YOU PANENKA IT INTO THE NET, ODD AND THE KEEPER SAVES IT!

ACTION! ➡ 51 MINS
You're hacked down in midfield, and the ref blows for a foul!

GOAL CHANCE! ➡ 53 MINS
You get another one-on-one!
EVENS DINKS IT OVER THE KEEPER, ROLL ODD AND YOU MISS IT!

GOAL? ➡ 55 MINS
Your defence gets sliced open!
EVENS SAVES THE SHOT, ODD AND YOU CONCEDE!

YELLOW CARD? ➡ 56 MINS
You slide in late!
EVENS GETS A WARNING, ROLL ODD FOR A BOOKING!

GOAL CHANCE! ➡ 58 MINS
You get on the end of a flick-on!
ROLL EVENS TO BURY IT, ROLL ODD TO MISS A TOTAL SITTER!

OFFSIDE! ⬇ 60 MINS
You dart in between the centre-backs, but stray offside!

⬅ ACTION! 61 MINS
You pick out your striker with a through ball, but they're shackled by the defender!

⬅ GOAL? 63 MINS
You give away a penalty!
ROLL EVENS FOR YOUR GOALIE TO SAVE IT, ROLL ODD AND IT'S A GOAL!

⬅ ACTION! 64 MINS
You fly past your marker down the left wing and whip in a quality cross!

⬅ INJURY? 65 MINS
You're tackled really late!
EVENS SKIPS THE TACKLE, ODD AND YOU TURN YOUR ANKLE!

⬅ ACTION! 67 MINS
You win the ball at the back and bring it out of defence!

⬇ ACTION! 68 MINS
You keep it simple and pass to your full-back!

GOAL CHANCE! ➡ 70 MINS
You hit a free-kick!
EVENS CURLS IT INTO THE TOP CORNER, ROLL ODD TO HIT THE WALL!
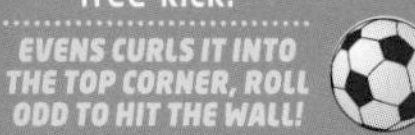

SUBS! ➡ 73 MINS
Time for a change!
ROLL EVENS TO ESCAPE BEING SUBBED, ROLL ODD TO BE TAKEN OFF!

ACTION! ➡ 75 MINS
You fly in for a 50-50 challenge!

YELLOW CARD? ➡ 77 MINS
You shout at the ref!
EVENS GETS A WARNING, ROLL ODD FOR A BOOKING!

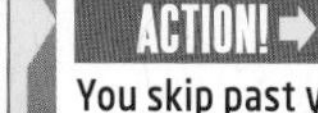

ACTION! ➡ 79 MINS
You skip past your marker, but they come back to tackle you!

ACTION! ⬇ 81 MINS
You play a quality one-two with your forward but the keeper smothers at your feet!

⬅ GOAL CHANCE! 82 MINS
You get a one-on-one!
ROLL EVENS TO SCORE, ROLL ODD TO FLUFF IT AND PUT IT WIDE!

⬅ RED CARD? 84 MINS
Your team gets hit on the break!
ROLL EVENS TO STOP THEM, ODD AND YOU SEE RED FOR DOGSO!

⬅ GOAL CHANCE! 85 MINS
Your winger whips in a wicked cross!
ROLL EVENS TO SCORE, ROLL ODD TO MISS!

⬅ ACTION! 87 MINS
You have a tussle in the middle of the park with the opposition's best midfielder!

⬅ GOAL CHANCE? 89 MINS
You score, but the opposition appeal for handball!
EVENS IS A GOAL, ODD AND VAR RULES IT OUT!

FINAL WHISTLE! 90 MINS
The Women's Euros final has finished!
DID YOU WIN THE MATCH?

HENRY

1 True or False? The all-time Arsenal legend was France's top scorer when they hosted and won the 1998 World Cup!

2 He starred in the Euro 2000 final as Les Bleus won another trophy. Who did they beat in the final?

3 Who did he replace as France's all-time top goalscorer in 2007 - David Trezeguet, Michel Platini or Zinedine Zidane?

4 And which fellow former Arsenal forward has since replaced Henry as Les Bleus' all-time top scorer?

5 How many caps did Henry win for his country between 1997 and 2010 - more or less than 100?

ANSWERS ON PAGE 94

LAMINE YAMAL

MATCH is here to tell you about the young stars that are getting ready to take over the global game...

WHO?

Lamine Yamal, the super talented teenager who has taken Barcelona and Spain by storm, becoming a key player for both club and country before turning 17!

WHAT'S SO GOOD ABOUT HIM?

Yamal has everything you could want from a winger. He's quick, sick at dribbling, and has a sweet left foot that can pick out a pass, drill in a cross or smash the ball into the back of the net! But the best thing about him is his brain – he always makes the right decisions, even though he's so inexperienced!

IN NUMBERS!

15 Age of Yamal when he made his Barcelona debut, making him the club's youngest player in 101 years!

16 Age when he became Spain's youngest-ever player and goalscorer too, breaking the record held by his team-mate Gavi!

£840M Value of the release clause in Yamal's Barca contract – that's how much a club would have to pay to sign him!

10 Goals and assists combined that Yamal bagged in La Liga in 2023-24 – scoring five and creating five!

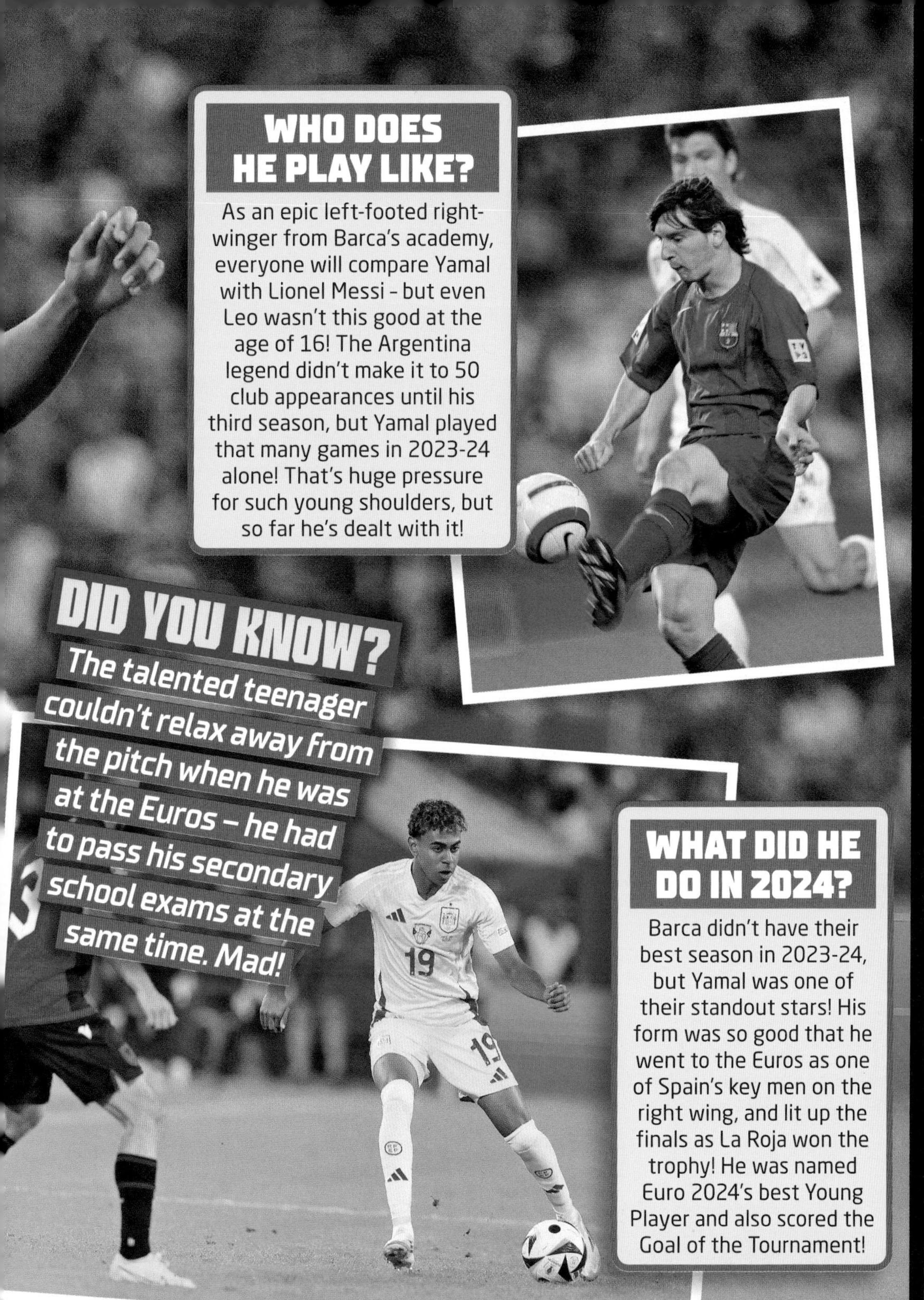

WHO DOES HE PLAY LIKE?

As an epic left-footed right-winger from Barca's academy, everyone will compare Yamal with Lionel Messi – but even Leo wasn't this good at the age of 16! The Argentina legend didn't make it to 50 club appearances until his third season, but Yamal played that many games in 2023-24 alone! That's huge pressure for such young shoulders, but so far he's dealt with it!

DID YOU KNOW?

The talented teenager couldn't relax away from the pitch when he was at the Euros – he had to pass his secondary school exams at the same time. Mad!

WHAT DID HE DO IN 2024?

Barca didn't have their best season in 2023-24, but Yamal was one of their standout stars! His form was so good that he went to the Euros as one of Spain's key men on the right wing, and lit up the finals as La Roja won the trophy! He was named Euro 2024's best Young Player and also scored the Goal of the Tournament!

WHAT'S NEXT?

Hansi Flick, Barca's new coach for 2024-25, has a lot of problems to fix, but his first job will be to build an exciting new team with all the club's young talent – and Yamal will be at the heart of it! He's attracting a lot of interest, but Barca are determined to keep hold of the teenager – gossips say they've already turned down a bid of £200m from PSG for him!

TEARAWAY TEENS!

Lamine Yamal isn't the only teenager to break through at a big club recently...

PAU CUBARSI

Barcelona & Spain

Yamal's 17-year-old team-mate came into Barca's defence in 2023-24, and the centre-back looked like he'd been there for years. Hero!

ARDA GULER

Real Madrid & Turkey

Real snapped up Guler in 2023, and at Euro 2024 he showed why with a worldy long-range curler in his first game v Georgia!

KOBBIE MAINOO

Man. United & England

We're not even exaggerating when we say that Mainoo is already one of The Red Devils' best players at the age of 19!

ARCHIE GRAY

Tottenham & England

After bossing the Championship with Leeds, Spurs paid £30m to sign the talented midfielder - and MATCH reckons that'll be a bargain!

WARREN ZAIRE-EMERY

PSG & France

After the departure of Kylian Mbappe, Zaire-Emery is getting ready to become the French champions' new local legend!

GUILLAUME RESTES

Toulouse & France

Most goalkeepers peak when they're in their 30s, but Restes was one of the best keepers in Ligue 1 last season at the age of 19!

BIG MATCH QUIZ!

How many of these epic Premier League teasers can you get right?

WHO STARTED WHERE?

Match these players with the clubs they started at!

OLLIE WATKINS	MOHAMMED KUDUS	ANTONEE ROBINSON	JOE GOMEZ	JAN PAUL VAN HECKE	VITALY JANELT

1

2

3

4

5

6

A

NORDSJAELLAND

B

CHARLTON

C

EXETER

D

RB LEIPZIG

E

EVERTON

F

NAC BREDA

job swap!

Which Prem star has switched careers to become an electrician?

LEGENDARY

Which sides did these past players play the most games for in their Prem career?

1. Yakubu
2. Jimmy Floyd Hasselbaink
3. Kevin Nolan
4. Juninho
5. Dimitar Berbatov
6. Robbie Fowler

FLAG FINDER!

Name this 2023-24 Premier League team from their players' nationalities!

ACE ACTIVITY

FOOTY MISMATCH

Can you spot ten differences between these 2023-24 pics?

ANSWERS ON PAGE 94

FOLLOW MATCH!

FOR LOADS OF AWESOME FOOTY NEWS, TRANSFER GOSSIP, VIDEOS & BANTER!

instagram.com/matchmagofficial

tiktok.com/matchmagofficial

X.com/matchmagazine

facebook.com/matchmagazine

You Tube

youtube.com/matchymovie

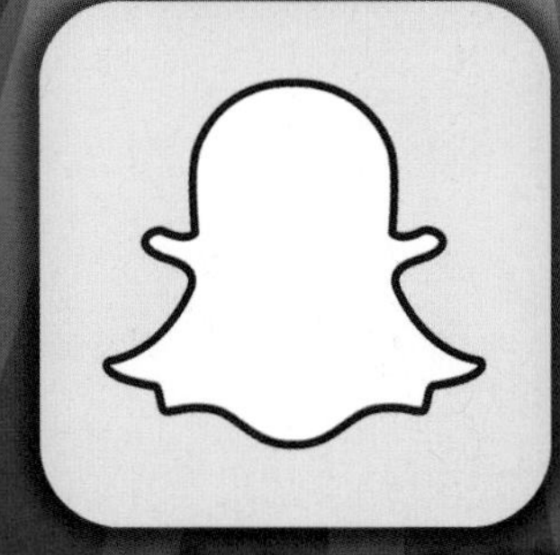

snapchat.com/add/matchmagazine

CHECK OUT MATCH ON SOCIAL MEDIA RIGHT NOW!

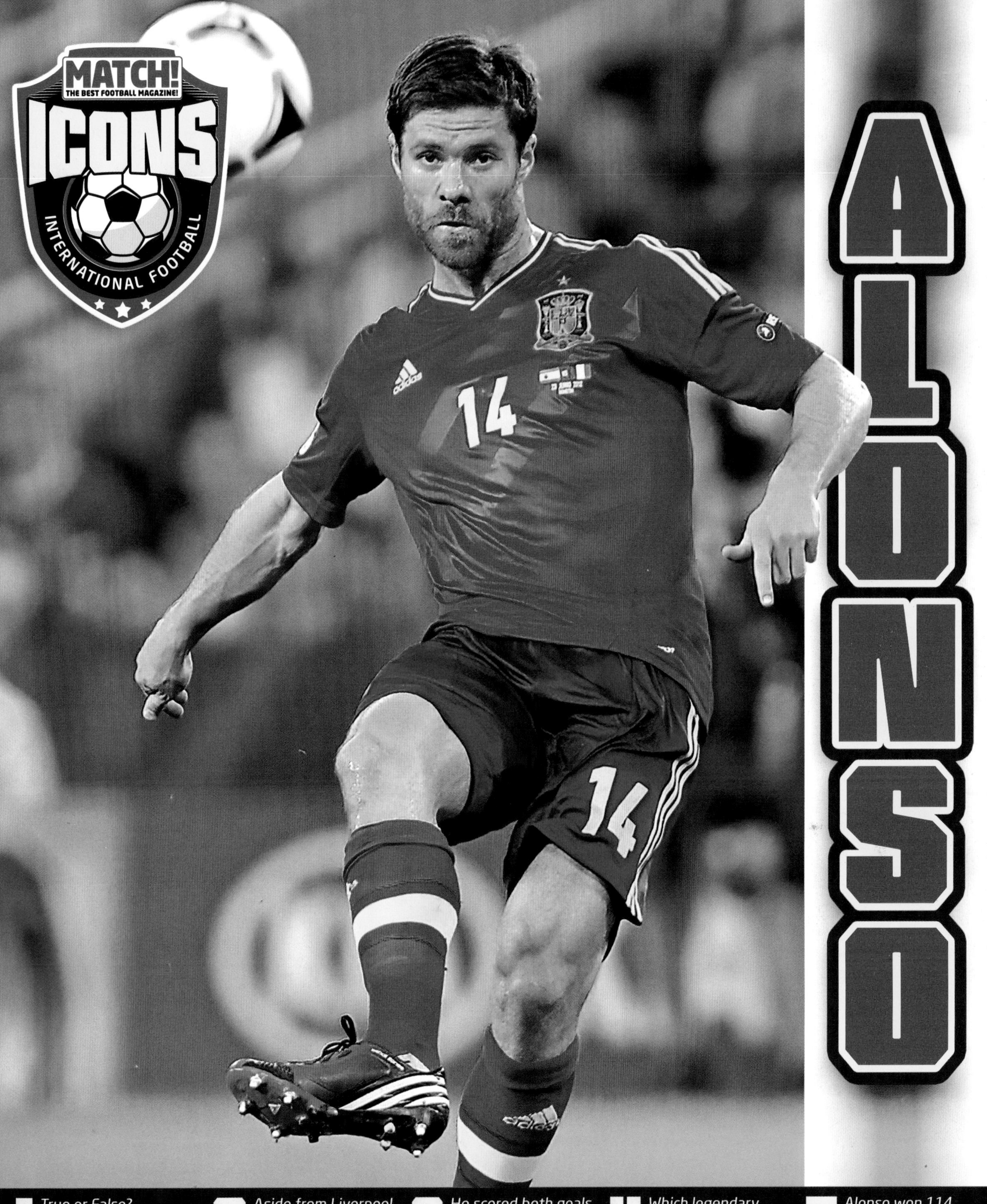

1 True or False? The former Liverpool midfielder started all seven games as Spain won the 2010 World Cup!

2 Aside from Liverpool, the silky Spaniard also played for Real Madrid, Real Sociedad, Eibar and which German club?

3 He scored both goals in Spain's Euro 2012 quarter-final victory against which side - France, Netherlands or Germany?

4 Which legendary midfielder won more caps for La Roja - Alonso, Andres Iniesta, Xavi or Cesc Fabregas?

5 Alonso won 114 caps in total for Spain, but how many international goals did he score - six, 16, 26 or 36?

ANSWERS ON PAGE 94

JURGEN KLOPP'S... LIVERPOOL

JURGEN KLOPP went into Liverpool's list of legends after stepping down as manager at the end of the 2023-24 season! We take a look back at the best moments from his nine years in charge...

KLOPP'S ARRIVAL

When Klopp arrived at Liverpool in October 2015, The Reds were tenth in the Prem, hadn't won a league title for 25 years and had only qualified for the Champions League once in the previous five seasons! The German had his work cut out...

CUP FINAL HEARTACHE

It didn't take long for Liverpool to start playing Klopp's high-pressing attacking style. It was crazy and chaotic, but it also took them to two cup finals in his first season! Sadly for The Reds, they lost both – first against Man. City in the League Cup, then to Sevilla in the Europa League!

THE EGYPTIAN KING & VVD

The 2016-17 campaign was key for Klopp. By qualifying for the Champions League, Liverpool could attract top talent once again and, the following season, Klopp made two of the most important signings in the club's history – Mohamed Salah from Roma and Virgil van Dijk from Southampton!

CHAMPO LEAGUE FINALISTS

Before Van Dijk and Salah arrived, Klopp's Liverpool were exciting but inconsistent. But with the Dutchman dominating the defence and Mo banging goals in for fun, The Reds became one of the best sides in Europe, beating Prem rivals Man. City on the way to the 2018 Champions League final!

scrapbook!

KARIUS' KYIV CRISIS

The 2018 Champions League final saw Liverpool take on Real Madrid in Kyiv, Ukraine. The Reds made a disastrous start when Salah dislocated his shoulder in the first 30 minutes after a tussle with Real skipper Sergio Ramos, and things got even worse when their goalkeeper Loris Karius made two howlers in a 3-1 defeat!

FINAL-DAY FAILURE

Klopp began the 2018-19 season more determined than ever to bring a trophy to Anfield, and added Brazil stars Alisson and Fabinho to his squad. His team were almost perfect in the Prem - racking up 97 points and only losing once all season - but still finished a point behind champions Man. City!

BARCA STUNNED AT ANFIELD

After losing 3-0 to Barcelona in the first leg of their 2018-19 Champions League semi-final, Liverpool needed a miracle in the second leg - and that's exactly what they got! Two goals each for fans' faves Divock Origi and Gini Wijnaldum inside a deafening Anfield stunned Barca and took Liverpool to Madrid for the final!

CHAMPIONS LEAGUE WINNERS

Liverpool were favourites when they faced Prem rivals Tottenham in the 2019 CL final, but Klopp was under pressure - he'd already lost three European finals with Borussia Dortmund and Liverpool! But an early Salah penalty helped settle his nerves, and a late Origi goal sealed the win!

TOP OF THE WORLD

Winning the Champions League meant that Liverpool qualified for the 2019 Club World Cup in Qatar, where they met Brazilian giants Flamengo in the final. After a nervous 90 minutes, Roberto Firmino bagged the extra-time winner as Klopp and his team were crowned kings of the world!

PREMIER LEAGUE CHAMPIONS

By 2020, it was 30 years since Liverpool last won a league title, but Klopp made sure that The Reds' supporters wouldn't have to wait any longer. His team dominated the 2019-20 season from day one and eventually finished 18 points clear at the top – the only downside was that they couldn't celebrate with their fans due to COVID!

ALISSON HEROICS

The 2020-21 campaign was a real low point for Liverpool. They had loads of injuries and never looked like defending their Prem title, but a late run of form took them into the top four. The best moment was a dramatic 2-1 win at West Brom, when goalkeeper Alisson came up for a corner to nod home the winner!

CUP DOUBLE

The 2021-22 season had the potential to be one of the best in Liverpool's history. In February they beat Chelsea on penalties in the League Cup final, then did exactly the same thing again three months later in the FA Cup final – setting them up for a shot of winning four trophies!

QUADRUPLE DREAMS DASHED

For the second time in Klopp's reign, Liverpool racked up more than 90 points to take the Premier League title race to the last day of the season – but once again, Man. City held on to win the league! A few days later, The Reds missed out on another huge honour, losing 1-0 to Real Madrid in the Champions League final. Gutted!

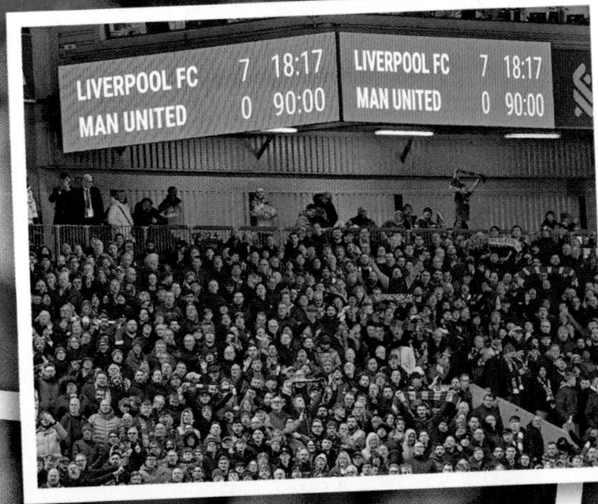

UNITED EMBARRASSED

The 2022-23 season was a tough one for Klopp as Liverpool finished fifth in the Premier League, but it still had some memorable moments. The high point was thrashing arch-rivals Man. United 7-0 at Anfield – the biggest-ever victory in the history of the fixture!

STEPPING DOWN

On January 26, 2024, Klopp stunned Liverpool fans and the rest of the footy world by announcing that the 2023-24 season would be his last at Anfield! Having won eight trophies in eight years, the German was desperate to go out on a high, and add a couple more...

ONE LAST TROPHY

Of all Klopp's finals, the 2023-24 League Cup was possibly the most dramatic! Liverpool were missing loads of first-team players to injury but, with the help of their academy stars, they managed to seal a 1-0 win over Chelsea with a header from skipper Virgil van Dijk!

THE NEXT BIG THING...

LINDA CAICEDO

MATCH is here to tell you about the young stars that are getting ready to take over the global game...

WHO?

Linda Caicedo, the 19-year-old Real Madrid and Colombia forward who's on track to become one of the greatest female footballers of all time!

WHAT'S SO GOOD ABOUT HER?

Caicedo made her senior debut in Colombia at the age of 14 and was one of the best players straight away – in her first season, she was the league's top scorer as her team America de Cali won the title! By the time she turned 17, she'd won another Golden Boot, this time in the Copa Libertadores, and reached a Copa America final for Colombia where she was named Player of the Tournament!

DID YOU KNOW?

Caicedo's sick solo effort against Germany at the 2023 World Cup was named Goal of the Tournament!

IN NUMBERS!

2 Clubs in Cali that Caicedo has played for – she started at America de Cali before leaving for their fierce rivals Deportivo Cali!

4 Goals Caicedo scored at the 2022 Under-17 World Cup, finishing joint-top of the scoring charts, as Colombia reached the final!

3 Number of World Cups Caicedo played in the space of one year between 2022 and 2023 – the Under-17s, Under-20s and senior tournament!

2 In 2023, Caicedo became only the second winner of the Golden Girl award – handed to the world's best player aged under 21!

WHO DOES SHE PLAY LIKE?

Caicedo's flair and quick-dancing feet leave defenders looking like statues – just like six-time World Player of the Year Marta! The Brazil legend retired from international football in 2024, but Caicedo is ready to replace her as the most exciting entertainer to watch at Women's World Cups!

WHAT DID SHE DO IN 2024?

2023-24 was Caicedo's first full season in Spain, but Real finished way behind Barcelona in the league and struggled in Europe despite Caicedo getting plenty of goals and assists. In February, she played in the CONCACAF W Gold Cup and scored twice as Colombia reached the quarter-finals, losing to hosts USA!

WHAT'S NEXT?

If Real are to close the gap on Barca, Caicedo will be key. With Spanish World Cup winners Olga Carmona and Athenea del Castillo alongside her, plus Denmark star Signe Bruun and French youngster Naomie Feller, they could build one of the most exciting teams in Europe!

RISING TALENTS!

Check out some of the other starlets with huge potential in the women's game...

TRINITY RODMAN
Washington Spirit & USA

The mega exciting USWNT attacker looks destined for sporting greatness – her dad, Dennis, was a basketball legend in the 1990s!

KYRA COONEY-CROSS
Arsenal & Australia

The midfielder hardly missed a minute in her country's run to the 2023 WC semi-finals, and bagged a move to Arsenal straight after!

ESMEE BRUGTS
Barcelona & Netherlands

Another young star that joined a big club after lighting up the World Cup Down Under in 2023, Brugts has a huge future in Barca's frontline!

MELCHIE DUMORNAY
Lyon & Haiti

Eight-time Champions League winners Lyon snapped up the Haiti attacking midfielder after she broke through at fellow French club Reims!

AGGIE BEEVER-JONES
Chelsea & England

Only Lauren James scored more goals for Chelsea than Beever-Jones last season, as The Blues won anothe Women's Super League title!

LILY YOHANNES
Ajax & USA

The youngest player in the history of the Women's Champions League scored within ten minutes of her USA debut at the age of 16 in March 2024!

BIG MATCH QUIZ!

How many of these wicked Euro leagues teasers can you get right?

NAME THE TEAM!

Can you name Barca's CL side that started against Napoli in February 2024?

1. GERMANY ★ GOALKEEPER

2. FRANCE ★ RIGHT-BACK

3. DENMARK ★ CENTRE-BACK

POLAND ★ STRIKER
ROBERT LEWANDOWSKI

4. URUGUAY ★ CENTRE-BACK

5. SPAIN ★ CENTRE-BACK

6. PORTUGAL ★ LEFT-BACK

7. SPAIN ★ MIDFIELDER

8. SPAIN ★ FORWARD

9. GERMANY ★ MIDFIELDER

10. NETHERLANDS ★ MIDFIELDER

NAME THE YEAR!

Can you remember what year all of these quality things happened?

- Gonzalo Higuain's 36 goals for Napoli equals the Serie A scoring record!
- Zlatan Ibrahimovic wins Ligue 1's top goalscorer prize with PSG!
- Pep Guardiola wins the Bundesliga title with Bayern Munich!

MATCH! WINNER!

Name the star whose epic match-winning hat-trick secured the 2024 Spanish Super Cup for Real Madrid!

FIVE-A-SIDE!

Can you work out which players are in this European Five-a-side team?

1. French goalkeeper who left Nottingham Forest for Lens in 2022!
2. Dutch defender currently playing for Spanish side Girona!
3. Ultra-silky Bayer Leverkusen attacking midfielder!
4. Real Madrid's French midfielder previously at Rennes!
5. Dutch targetman who top scored for PSV in 2023-24!

ACE ACTIVITY

FACE IN THE CROWD

Find 10 European-based superstars in this crazy Real Madrid crowd!

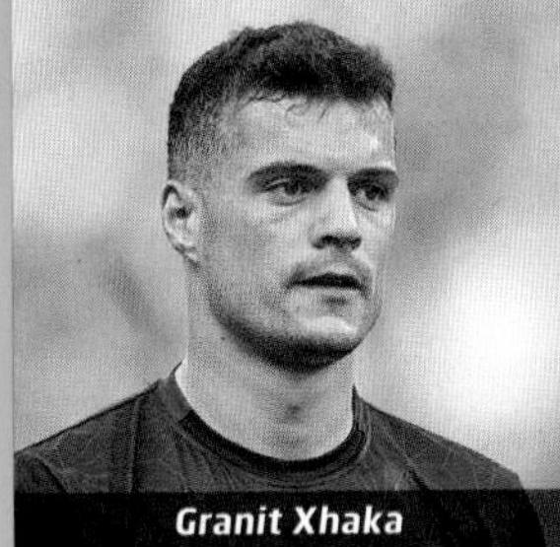
Granit Xhaka

Lautaro Martinez

Douglas Luiz

Aurelien Tchouameni

Julian Alvarez

Isco

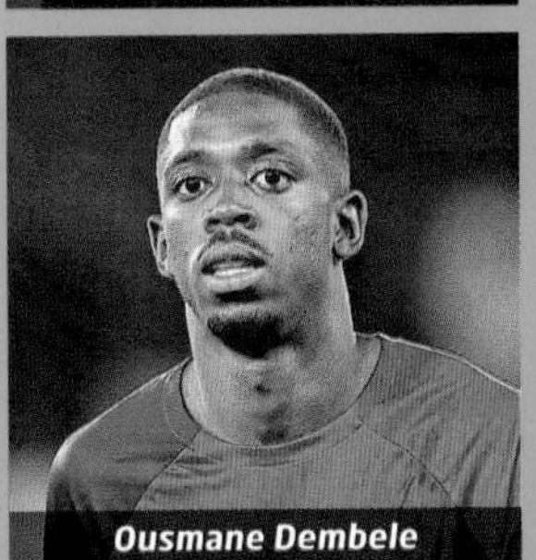
Ousmane Dembele

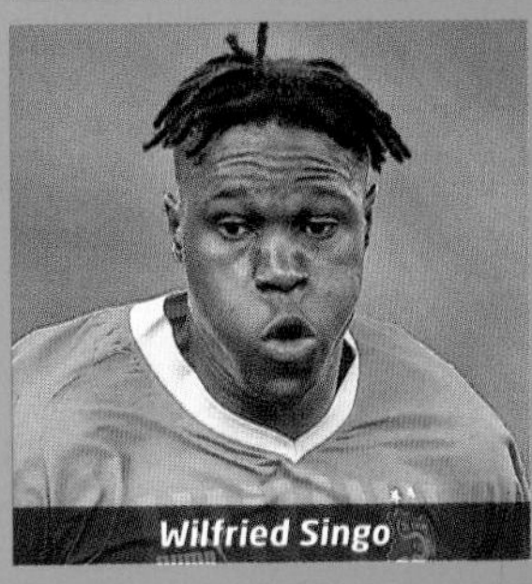
Wilfried Singo

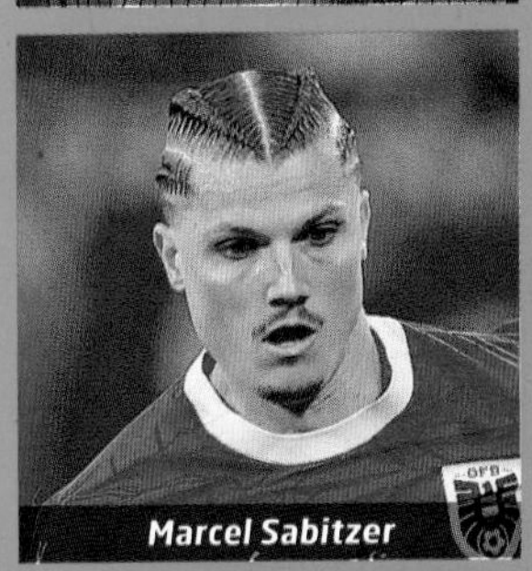
Marcel Sabitzer

Rafael Leao

ANSWERS ON PAGE 94

ULTIMATE PLAYER!

MATCH picks the best Premier League players over the past year to help create the league's ultimate star – and then we want you to do the same! Check out our elite shortlist, then get thinking!

These eagle-eyed ballers can play passes and unlock defences like no other!

BRUNO GUIMARAES
MIDFIELDER ★ NEWCASTLE

The Magpies midfielder's vision is so good, he doesn't just pass every eye exam - he could open his own opticians! Best mate Joelinton would get a free pair of specs, of course!

MY PICK

MY PICK

ENZO FERNANDEZ
MIDFIELDER ★ CHELSEA

One of the most important lessons when learning to be a midfielder is to keep your head up - just like Enzo does! It's the busiest area of the pitch and things can change mega fast, so you need to know what's around you!

BRUNO FERNANDES
MIDFIELDER ★ MAN. UNITED

Red Devils fans should nickname Bruno "The Printer", because he's constantly scanning the pitch! It means he always has a mental picture of what's around him, so he can easily "photocopy" an assist for a team-mate. LOL!

MY PICK

PHIL FODEN
MIDFIELDER ★ MAN. CITY

All it takes is one quick glance over his shoulder for Foden to have an entire visual map of what's going on behind him! That comes in well handy when he has defenders charging in to tackle him!

MY PICK

ALEXIS MAC ALLISTER
MIDFIELDER ★ LIVERPOOL

Your teachers might threaten that they have "eyes in the back of their heads", but we reckon the Reds midfielder actually might! He seems to know exactly where his team-mates are at all times!

MY PICK

HEADING

These superstars barely ever get beaten in the air – they're proper aerial beasts!

TOMAS SOUCEK

MIDFIELDER ★ WEST HAM

The 6ft 4in giant CM maybe doesn't win quite as many headers as a centre-back or striker would, but that's only because long balls often bypass him in midfield! His aerial duels success rate is actually incredible, though!

MY PICK ☐

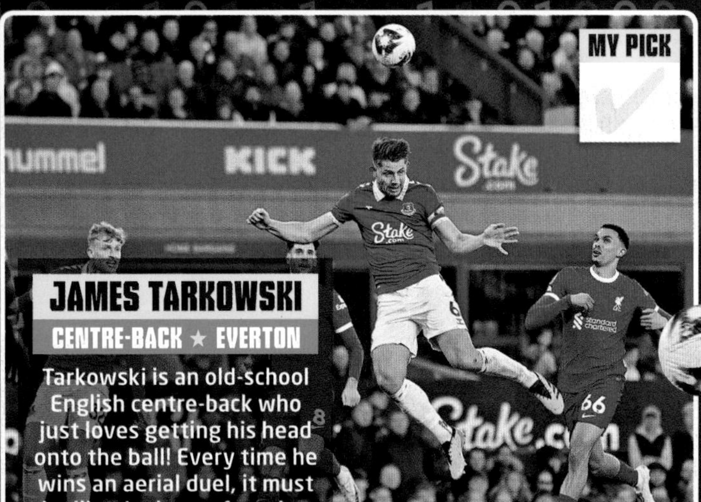

MY PICK ☐

JAMES TARKOWSKI

CENTRE-BACK ★ EVERTON

Tarkowski is an old-school English centre-back who just loves getting his head onto the ball! Every time he wins an aerial duel, it must be like the buzz of scoring a goal for the defender!

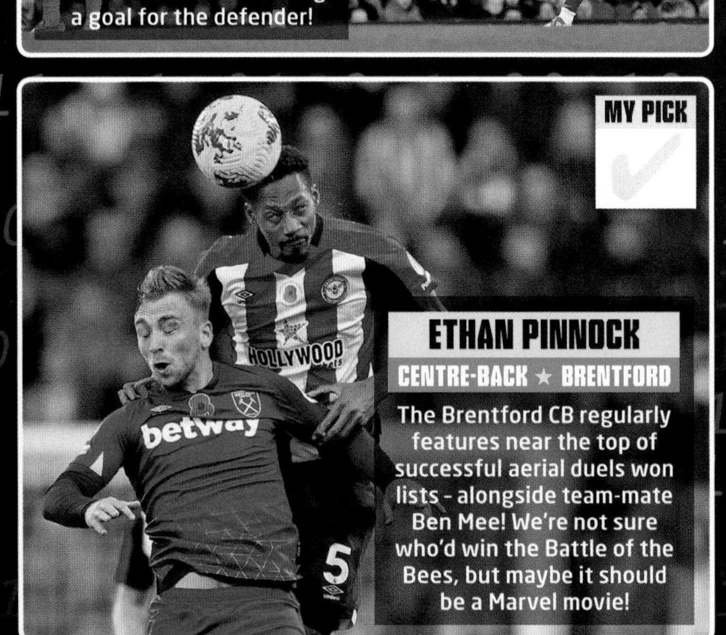

MY PICK ☐

ETHAN PINNOCK

CENTRE-BACK ★ BRENTFORD

The Brentford CB regularly features near the top of successful aerial duels won lists - alongside team-mate Ben Mee! We're not sure who'd win the Battle of the Bees, but maybe it should be a Marvel movie!

MY PICK ☐

DOMINIC SOLANKE

STRIKER ★ TOTTENHAM

If you studied his entire career stats, Solanke hasn't scored as many headers as you'd expect him to have done! That doesn't take away from the fact that he can rise like a London tower block!

MY PICK ☐

HARRY MAGUIRE

CENTRE-BACK ★ MAN. UNITED

Maguire's first-ever England goal was a header at the 2018 World Cup - and popping up with important headed goals has become a speciality throughout his career ever since. Legend!

FREE-KICKS

Beware making a foul – these dead-ball demons can rip the net from any distance!

HARRY WILSON

WINGER ★ FULHAM

He hasn't scored as many in recent seasons, but Wilson established himself as a fabulous free-kick taker at the start of his career! He scored five in all comps in 2019-20 while on loan at Derby and two in one game for Cardiff in 2020-21 against Birmingham. Welsh wizard!

MY PICK

EBERECHI EZE

MIDFIELDER ★ C. PALACE

Can you remember Eze's free-kick against Tottenham last season? Even though Guglielmo Vicario was standing in the right place, he still had no chance of keeping the thunderbolt out. Worldy alert!

MY PICK

JAMES WARD-PROWSE

MIDFIELDER ★ WEST HAM

JWP's idol growing up was David Beckham, and they just so happen to be the Premier League's all-time top two scoring free-kick takers! They can both claim to be the PL's GOAT free-kick taker!

MY PICK

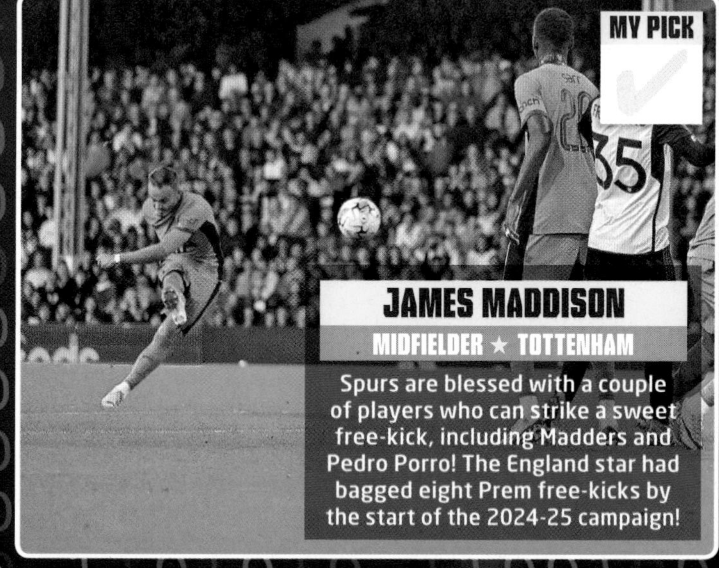

JAMES MADDISON

MIDFIELDER ★ TOTTENHAM

Spurs are blessed with a couple of players who can strike a sweet free-kick, including Madders and Pedro Porro! The England star had bagged eight Prem free-kicks by the start of the 2024-25 campaign!

MY PICK

MARCUS RASHFORD

FORWARD ★ MAN. UNITED

Rashford is one of the best finishers in the league, so it's no surprise that he can hit a mean free-kick too! He also has tons of variety - sometimes he'll bend it and sometimes he'll go for a mind-blowing knuckleball!

MY PICK

POWER

When the footy skills wear off, these guys could join WWE! Don't mess with 'em!

SVEN BOTMAN

CENTRE-BACK ★ NEWCASTLE

Any player nicknamed "Batman" is bound to have special powers! The mega classy Newcastle and Netherlands defender combines composure on the ball with strength!

CHRIS WOOD

STRIKER ★ NOTT'M FOREST

There are some strong lads at Forest, but the Kiwi can outmuscle most! His immense upper-body strength is his biggest weapon when it comes to holding up the play for his side!

NICLAS FULLKRUG

STRIKER ★ WEST HAM

Fullkrug is like a human trampoline, because players just bounce off him! A hard shoulder-to-shoulder with the Hammers giant is very likely to end with the opposition on their backside!

ADAMA TRAORE

WINGER ★ FULHAM

Adama once said he didn't lift any weights to get his mega muscles, which he lathers up with baby oil before games so markers can't grab his arms! We'd love to know his secret - and yes, we've already tried Popeye's spinach technique!

GABRIEL

CENTRE-BACK ★ ARSENAL

When the Brazil beast retires from footy, he could definitely become a bouncer! His aggression and physique intimidates attackers, and he loves stopping them from getting into the no-go areas! We've hardly ever seen him get outmuscled!

TRICKS

These skillers wow the crowds with their amazing tricks and jaw-dropping tekkers!

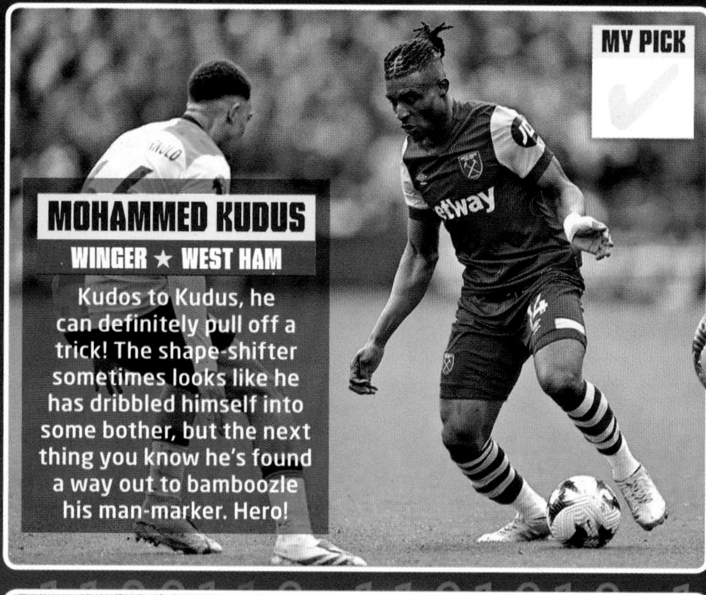

MY PICK

MOHAMMED KUDUS

WINGER ★ WEST HAM

Kudos to Kudus, he can definitely pull off a trick! The shape-shifter sometimes looks like he has dribbled himself into some bother, but the next thing you know he's found a way out to bamboozle his man-marker. Hero!

MY PICK

GABRIEL MARTINELLI

WINGER ★ ARSENAL

Martinelli's wing wizardry would make Harry Potter blush! The Gunners superstar doesn't need a broomstick to make it look like he's flying past a defender either!

MY PICK

CHRISTOPHER NKUNKU

FORWARD ★ CHELSEA

Last season's injury woes were so unfair to Premier League fans, because we lost almost a whole season of Nkunku magic! We've genuinely seen him perform a double pirouette past two different defenders in the past. Mad!

MY PICK

LUIS DIAZ

WINGER ★ LIVERPOOL

There are some things in football you can teach to perfection, and others just come naturally to players! If only we could bottle up some of Diaz's flair and share it around, life would be fairer!

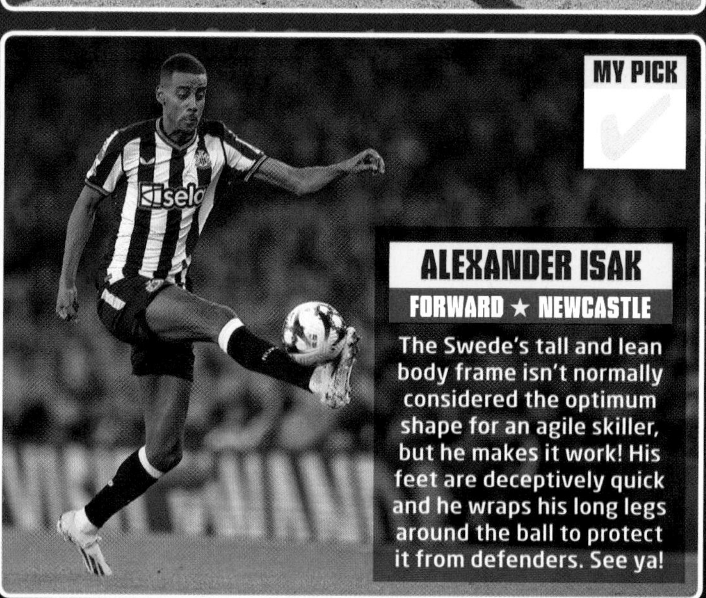

MY PICK

ALEXANDER ISAK

FORWARD ★ NEWCASTLE

The Swede's tall and lean body frame isn't normally considered the optimum shape for an agile skiller, but he makes it work! His feet are deceptively quick and he wraps his long legs around the ball to protect it from defenders. See ya!

WORK-RATE

These lung-busters' batteries are always fully charged – they can run all day!

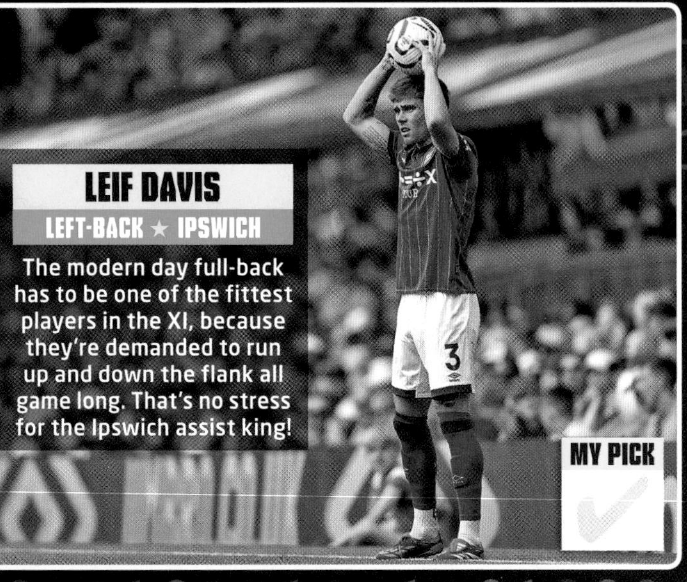

LEIF DAVIS

LEFT-BACK ★ IPSWICH

The modern day full-back has to be one of the fittest players in the XI, because they're demanded to run up and down the flank all game long. That's no stress for the Ipswich assist king!

MY PICK ☐

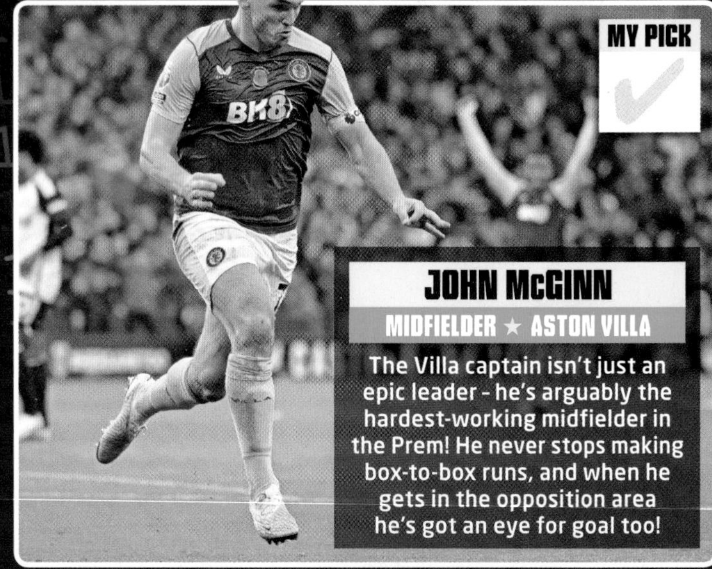

JOHN McGINN

MIDFIELDER ★ ASTON VILLA

The Villa captain isn't just an epic leader - he's arguably the hardest-working midfielder in the Prem! He never stops making box-to-box runs, and when he gets in the opposition area he's got an eye for goal too!

MY PICK ☐

DECLAN RICE

MIDFIELDER ★ ARSENAL

An easy way to win over a new set of fans is to give 100% every game - and that's exactly what Rice did in his debut campaign at Arsenal! He also ran more distance than anyone at Euro 2024!

MY PICK ☐

DEJAN KULUSEVSKI

WINGER ★ TOTTENHAM

The silky Swede isn't just great with the ball at his feet, he's also a tireless runner! The wing wizard covered 13.36km during Tottenham's 2-1 home win against Everton in 2023-24 - a record high for any Prem player in a single game last season!

MY PICK ☐

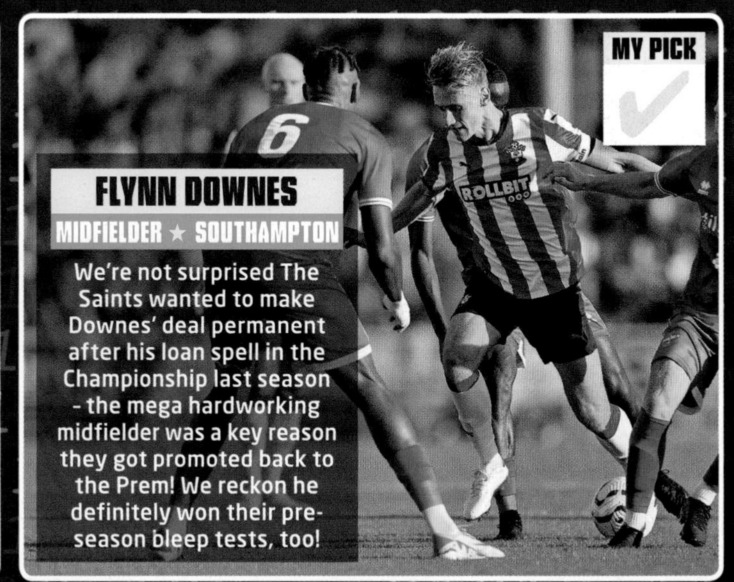

FLYNN DOWNES

MIDFIELDER ★ SOUTHAMPTON

We're not surprised The Saints wanted to make Downes' deal permanent after his loan spell in the Championship last season - the mega hardworking midfielder was a key reason they got promoted back to the Prem! We reckon he definitely won their pre-season bleep tests, too!

MY PICK ☐

FINISHING

Keepers don't stand a chance against these deadly hitmen! They only need a sniff of goal!

MY PICK

HEUNG-MIN SON

FORWARD ★ TOTTENHAM

We genuinely believe Son could have the best goal catalogue in Premier League history! Okay, so he doesn't score many headers, but he can bust net with either foot - and from close range or from outside the box. Legend!

MY PICK

ERLING HAALAND

STRIKER ★ MAN. CITY

Haaland scored 125 goals in his first 133 games in Europe's top five leagues for Borussia Dortmund and Man. City! That sort of scoring record is basically unheard of in football history!

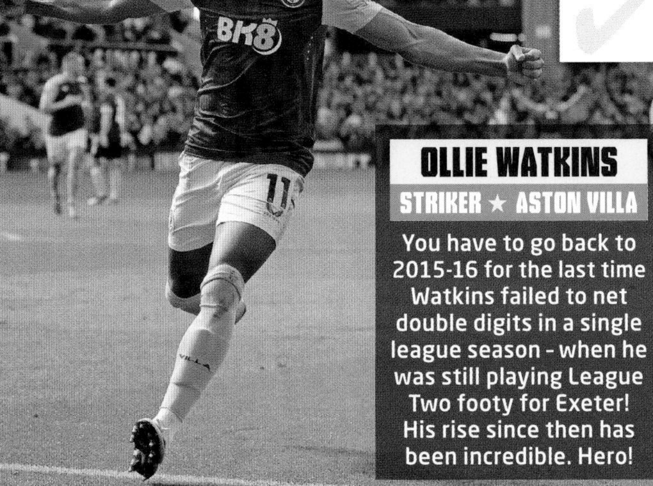

MY PICK

OLLIE WATKINS

STRIKER ★ ASTON VILLA

You have to go back to 2015-16 for the last time Watkins failed to net double digits in a single league season - when he was still playing League Two footy for Exeter! His rise since then has been incredible. Hero!

MOHAMED SALAH

FORWARD ★ LIVERPOOL

Salah's 31 non-penalty goals in 2017-18 is a joint all-time Premier League record alongside former Reds striker Luis Suarez! That's three more than Haaland's record-breaking 2022-23 tally, as eight of his goals were pens!

MY PICK

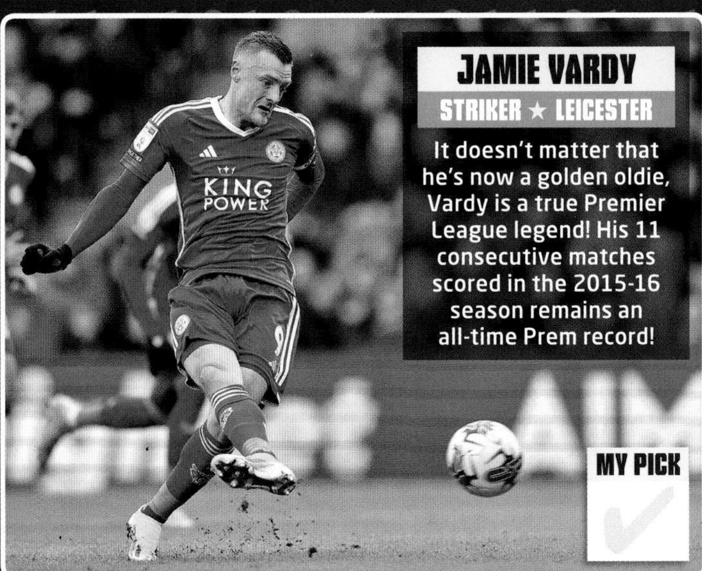

JAMIE VARDY

STRIKER ★ LEICESTER

It doesn't matter that he's now a golden oldie, Vardy is a true Premier League legend! His 11 consecutive matches scored in the 2015-16 season remains an all-time Prem record!

MY PICK

HANDS

These guys definitely don't have butter fingers or poppadom wrists!

JORDAN PICKFORD

GOALKEEPER ★ EVERTON

The Toffees and England goalkeeper is arguably the most agile keeper in the Premier League! He catapults himself across his goal and is one of only a few goalies to have won multiple Premier League Save of the Month awards!

MY PICK ✔

GUGLIELMO VICARIO

GOALKEEPER ★ TOTTENHAM

The Spurs shot-stopper is nicknamed after supervillain Venom, and it definitely feels like he has powers at times! He seems to gain an extra few inches - even when he appears to be at full stretch!

MY PICK ✔

ALISSON

GOALKEEPER ★ LIVERPOOL

You never really think about how important your fingertips are...unless you're a goalkeeper! You can't imagine how many times Alisson's fingertips have saved Liverpool from conceding a goal!

MY PICK ✔

DAVID RAYA

GOALKEEPER ★ ARSENAL

Arsenal were always going to make Raya's loan deal a permanent one after his heroic displays last season! He kept 16 clean sheets to win the Golden Glove - despite sharing minutes with Aaron Ramsdale at the start of the year!

MY PICK ✔

EDERSON

GOALKEEPER ★ MAN. CITY

The City keeper is widely recognised as being the best ball-playing goalkeeper on the planet, but that shouldn't take away from his shot-stopping ability! City supporters will never forget his last-gasp saves in the 2023 CL final!

MY PICK ✔

BRAIN

These stars are always one step ahead thanks to their epic footy intelligence!

KEVIN DE BRUYNE

MIDFIELDER ★ MAN. CITY

The highest ever IQ scores for human intelligence were around the 250 to 300 mark, but De Bruyne's footy IQ must be even higher! He never, ever makes the wrong decision - hence why he gets so many assists!

KOBBIE MAINOO

MIDFIELDER ★ MAN. UNITED

We still can't believe how young the United midfielder is, because he acts like he's an experienced veteran! His incredible composure on the ball isn't normal for a player of his age!

COLE PALMER

MIDFIELDER ★ CHELSEA

You can tell that Palmer progressed through the City academy at the same time that De Bruyne was at the club, because he has a lot of similar traits! He would have been the perfect long-term replacement for KDB!

DOMINIK SZOBOSZLAI

MIDFIELDER ★ LIVERPOOL

Historically, Hungary have had some of the most technical players on the planet - their team from the early 1950s is considered one of the best international teams of all time! You can tell Szobo definitely has that in his DNA!

MARTIN ODEGAARD

MIDFIELDER ★ ARSENAL

The Norway sensation was once considered a "boy genius" when he was snapped up by Real Madrid as a 16-year-old! Well...now he's an adult genius! You can tell he barely has to think when he has the ball at his feet. Master!

TACKLING

Tackle machine alert – these solid stars love stopping attackers in their tracks!

RUBEN DIAS

CENTRE-BACK ★ MAN. CITY

Because City have so much control of the ball, Dias doesn't generally get called into that many duels – but, when he does, it's rare that he loses out!

MY PICK

WILLIAM SALIBA

CENTRE-BACK ★ ARSENAL

Trying to dribble past Saliba is like trying to lick your own elbow, or read with your eyes shut...it's just not going to happen! Even if you did manage it once, he'd still use his explosive pace to catch up and recover!

MY PICK

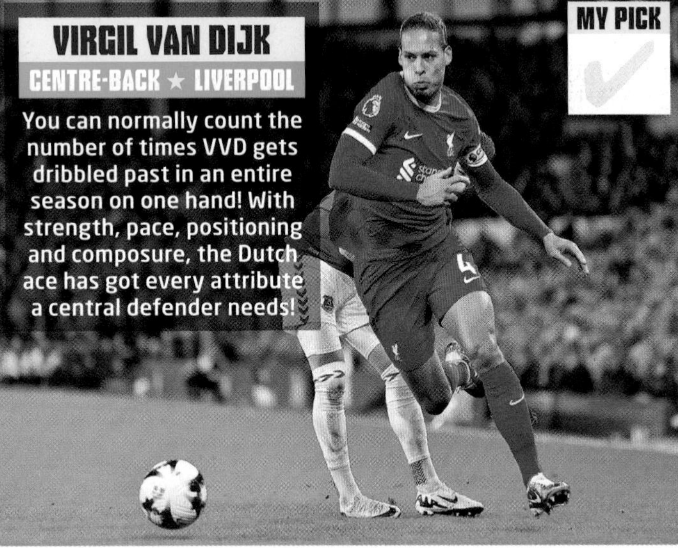

VIRGIL VAN DIJK

CENTRE-BACK ★ LIVERPOOL

You can normally count the number of times VVD gets dribbled past in an entire season on one hand! With strength, pace, positioning and composure, the Dutch ace has got every attribute a central defender needs!

MY PICK

JOAO GOMES

MIDFIELDER ★ WOLVES

A relative newbie to the Premier League, Wolves warrior Gomes has established himself as one of the snappiest tacklers in England! He's like a pitbull in midfield with his aggression and persistence!

MY PICK

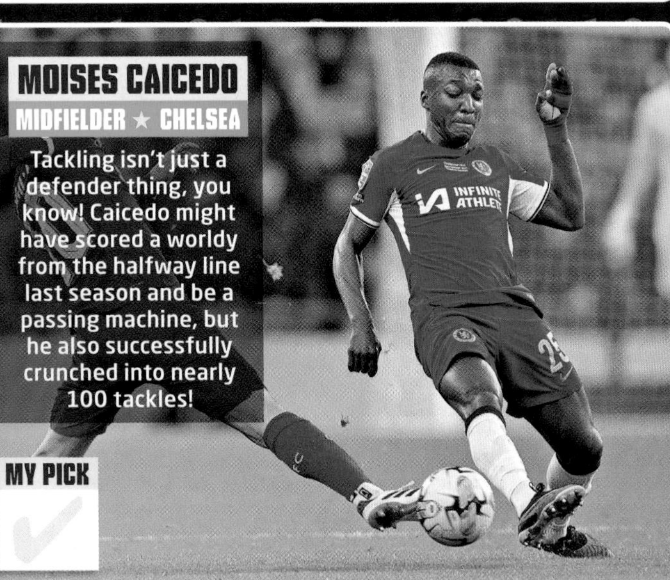

MOISES CAICEDO

MIDFIELDER ★ CHELSEA

Tackling isn't just a defender thing, you know! Caicedo might have scored a worldy from the halfway line last season and be a passing machine, but he also successfully crunched into nearly 100 tackles!

MY PICK

SPEED

These speedsters are like football's version of Formula 1 – they're absolutely lightning!

KYLE WALKER

RIGHT-BACK ★ MAN. CITY

Even though 34-year-old Walker is no spring chicken in footy terms, he still has the pace to burn past players who are ten years younger than him! Try to keep up, young blood!

MY PICK ✔

MICKY VAN DE VEN

CENTRE-BACK ★ TOTTENHAM

The main reason Spurs can play such a high line is because of Van de Ven's ridiculous recovery speed! He broke the all-time Premier League record for the fastest sprint at the start of 2024, reaching 37.38km/h!

MY PICK ✔

ANTHONY ELANGA

WINGER ★ NOTT'M FOREST

Van de Ven was the only current Premier League player to record a faster speed than Elanga last season! Electric pace is a particularly useful asset to have when running onto team-mate Chris Wood's flick-ons!

MY PICK ✔

PEDRO NETO

WINGER ★ CHELSEA

Neto is the very definition of a "nippy winger"! The fact that he can run almost as quickly with the ball as he can without it means he is the perfect player to launch on a counter-attack!

MY PICK ✔

ANTHONY GORDON

WINGER ★ NEWCASTLE

What do cheetahs, bullets, tornados, a peregrine falcon, the blink of an eye and Anthony Gordon have in common? They all feature on MATCH's list of the quickest things on the planet!

MY PICK ✔

DRIBBLING

Defenders dread one-on-ones with these dribble kings – the ball's glued to their feet!

JEREMY DOKU

WINGER ★ MAN. CITY

We're not surprised Doku loves the Griddy celebration, which involves dancing away in jubilation, because it's similar to the way he skips past opponents! There aren't many better one-v-one dribblers on the planet!

KAORU MITOMA

WINGER ★ BRIGHTON

Every time Mitoma gets on the ball, the crowd collectively holds their breath as they wait for something to happen! His dribble success rate is so good, you always expect him to beat his man!

MATHEUS CUNHA

FORWARD ★ WOLVES

This might take you by surprise, but only a few players completed more dribbles than Cunha in the Premier League in 2023-24! He's an underrated dribbler and an underrated skiller - he has some moves!

MY PICK

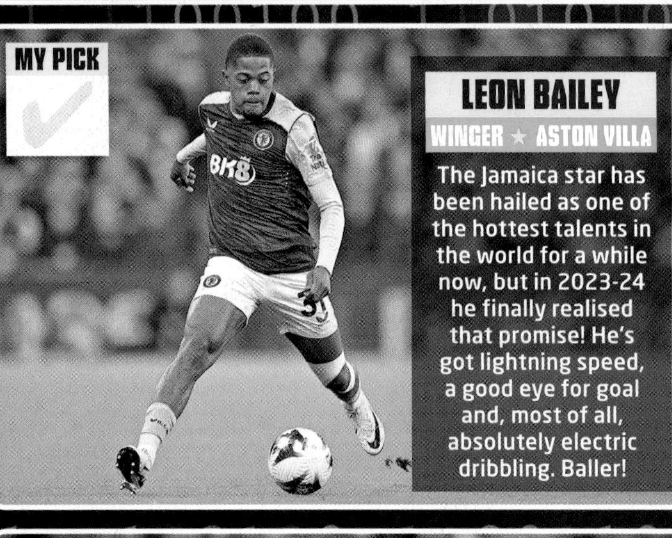

LEON BAILEY

WINGER ★ ASTON VILLA

The Jamaica star has been hailed as one of the hottest talents in the world for a while now, but in 2023-24 he finally realised that promise! He's got lightning speed, a good eye for goal and, most of all, absolutely electric dribbling. Baller!

BUKAYO SAKA

WINGER ★ ARSENAL

When Saka gets going, it's RIP for defenders' ankles! He's so direct and can flip-flap past defenders, moving the ball one way before quickly snapping back the other, just like an elastic band!

PASSING

These stars are made for playing possession footy – they never give it away!

RODRI

MIDFIELDER ★ MAN. CITY

Spanish midfielders have a history of being incredible passers - and Rodri is no exception! Since joining the Prem in 2018, he has completed over 13,800 passes...and counting!

MY PICK

MY PICK

HARRY WINKS

MIDFIELDER ★ LEICESTER

Winksy's transfer to Leicester was exactly the right move at exactly the right time! He completed more passes than any other midfielder in the Championship in 2023-24 with a remarkable 94% success rate!

LEWIS DUNK

CENTRE-BACK ★ BRIGHTON

You may associate the Seagulls skipper more with monster headers given his towering height, but he's actually the only player other than Rodri to clock up more than 6,000 passes over the past two seasons! He loves playing out from the back to launch attacks!

MY PICK

MY PICK

TRENT ALEXANDER-ARNOLD

RIGHT-BACK ★ LIVERPOOL

Forget Frodo and the Lord of the Rings, Alexander-Arnold is "Lord of the Pings!" The way he can launch a long-distance ball from the right-back position onto a forward player's feet is, well... "preciooous"!

JORGINHO

MIDFIELDER ★ ARSENAL

At all the clubs he has played for, Jorginho has been the beating heart of every midfield! He always makes himself an option for his team-mates and moves the ball quickly from one area of the pitch to the next, often passing forward and playing killer through balls!

MY PICK

BUILD YOUR ULTIMATE PLAYER

HEADING
MATCH PICKS:
JAMES TARKOWSKI
YOU PICK:
....

VISION
MATCH PICKS:
BRUNO FERNANDES
YOU PICK:
....

POWER
MATCH PICKS:
ADAMA TRAORE
YOU PICK:
....

FREE-KICKS
MATCH PICKS:
JAMES WARD-PROWSE
YOU PICK:
....

TRICKS
MATCH PICKS:
CHRISTOPHER NKUNKU
YOU PICK:
....

FINISHING
MATCH PICKS:
ERLING HAALAND
YOU PICK:
....

BRAIN
MATCH PICKS:
KEVIN DE BRUYNE
YOU PICK:
....

WORK-RATE
MATCH PICKS:
DECLAN RICE
YOU PICK:
....

HANDS
MATCH PICKS:
ALISSON
YOU PICK:
....

SPEED
MATCH PICKS:
MICKY VAN DE VEN
YOU PICK:
....

TACKLING
MATCH PICKS:
VIRGIL VAN DIJK
YOU PICK:
....

DRIBBLING
MATCH PICKS:
KAORU MITOMA
YOU PICK:
....

PASSING
MATCH PICKS:
RODRI
YOU PICK:
....

SEND IT IN!

Send us a photo of your Ultimate Player drawing and we'll feature the best ones in MATCH magazine and on our epic social media channels!

Email: match.magazine@kelsey.co.uk
facebook.com/matchmagazine
X.com/matchmagazine
instagram.com/matchmagofficial

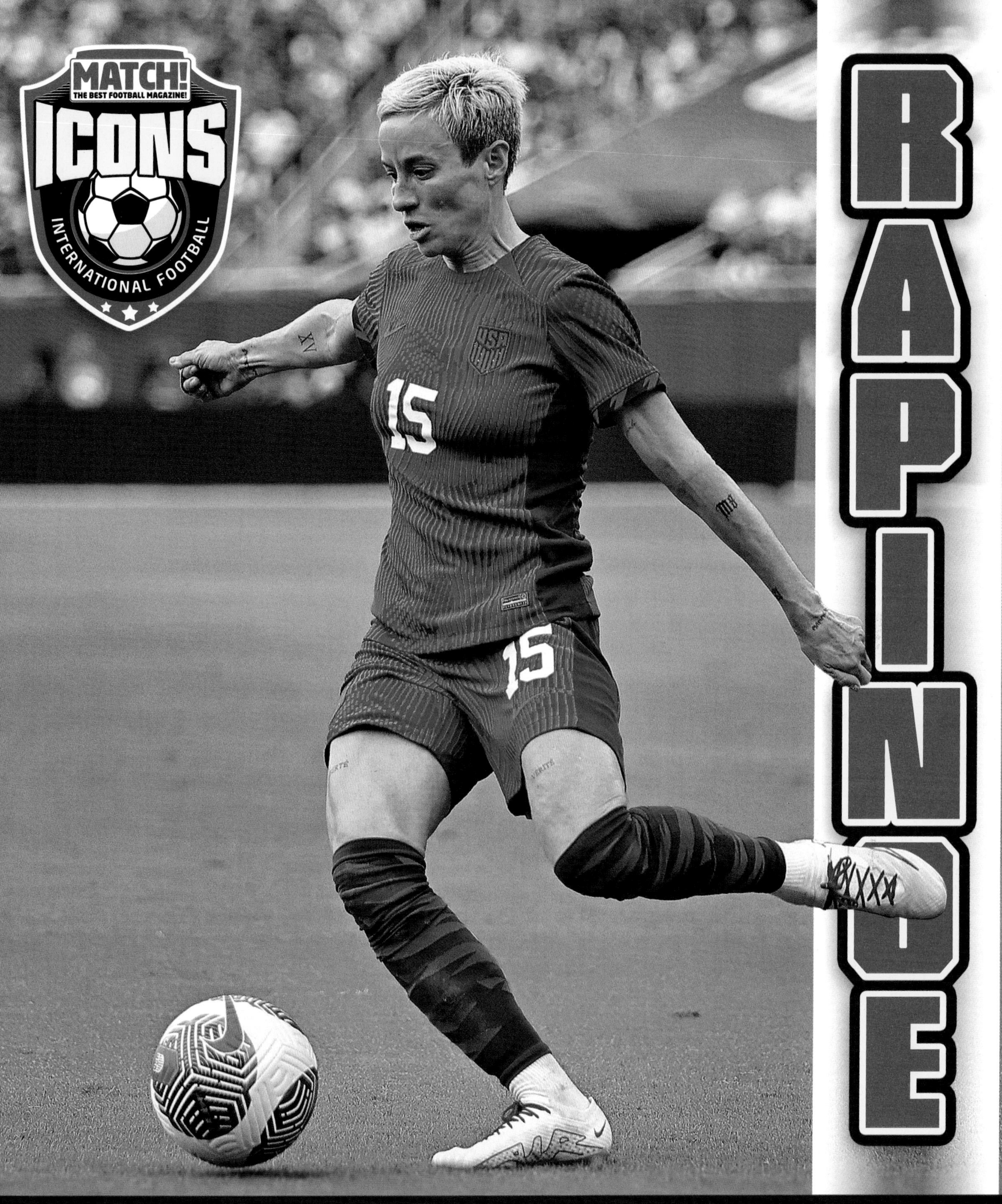

1 True or False? She is the only player, male or female, to score an Olimpico (a goal from a corner) at the Olympics!

2 The winger helped USA win the 2012 Olympics at what famous stadium - Wembley, the San Siro or Bernabeu?

3 In 2019 against the Netherlands, Rapinoe became the oldest woman to score in a World Cup final at what age?

4 As well as the Golden Boot for top scorer, what other individual prize did Megan win at the 2019 World Cup in France?

5 Which awesome boot brand did she wear throughout her epic career - Under Armour, adidas, Nike or Puma?

ANSWERS ON PAGE 94

BIG MATCH QUIZ!

How many of these mind-boggling EFL teasers can you get right?

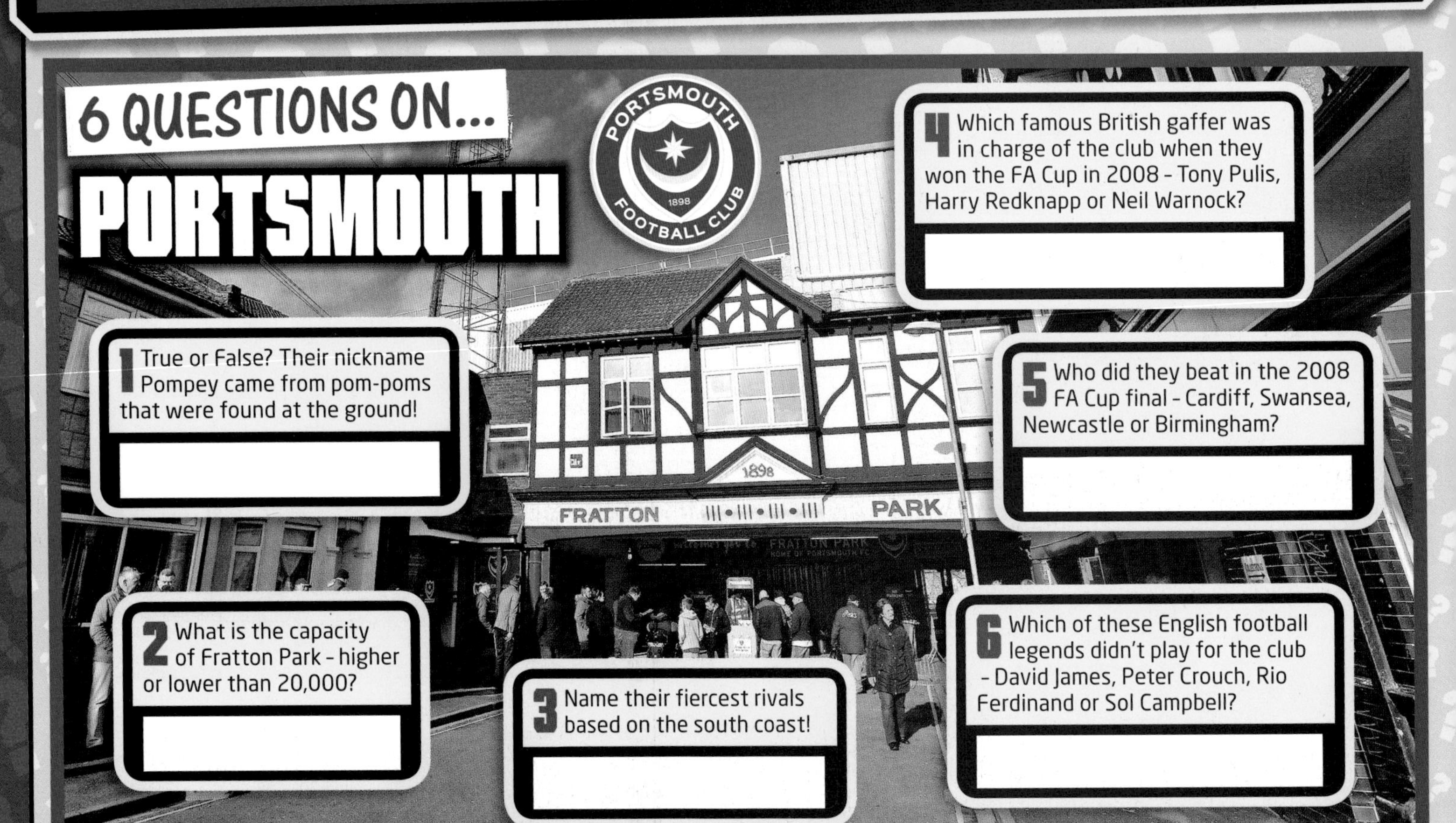

6 QUESTIONS ON... PORTSMOUTH

1 True or False? Their nickname Pompey came from pom-poms that were found at the ground!

2 What is the capacity of Fratton Park - higher or lower than 20,000?

3 Name their fiercest rivals based on the south coast!

4 Which famous British gaffer was in charge of the club when they won the FA Cup in 2008 - Tony Pulis, Harry Redknapp or Neil Warnock?

5 Who did they beat in the 2008 FA Cup final - Cardiff, Swansea, Newcastle or Birmingham?

6 Which of these English football legends didn't play for the club - David James, Peter Crouch, Rio Ferdinand or Sol Campbell?

Can you do the sums to get the answer to this maths question?

Number of Welsh clubs in the English Football League!

+

Number of teams in the English Football League Two!

−

Number of Championship clubs that had 'City' in their name in 2023-24!

=

ANSWER

FACE TO FACE

Can you name these two mixed up Championship megastars?

NAME THE CLUB!

Which Championship club's record is this over the past five seasons?

2023-24

2022-23

2021-22

2020-21 19TH

2019-20 12TH

ACE ACTIVITY

WORDFIT

Fit 20 English Football League clubs with animals in their badges in this huge grid!

- Bradford
- Bristol City
- Cardiff
- Cheltenham
- Derby
- Gillingham
- Hull
- Mansfield
- Middlesbrough
- Millwall
- Morecambe
- Norwich
- Oxford
- Sheffield Wednesday
- Swansea
- Swindon
- Walsall
- Watford
- West Brom
- Wycombe

SHEFFIELDWEDNESDAY

ANSWERS ON PAGE 94

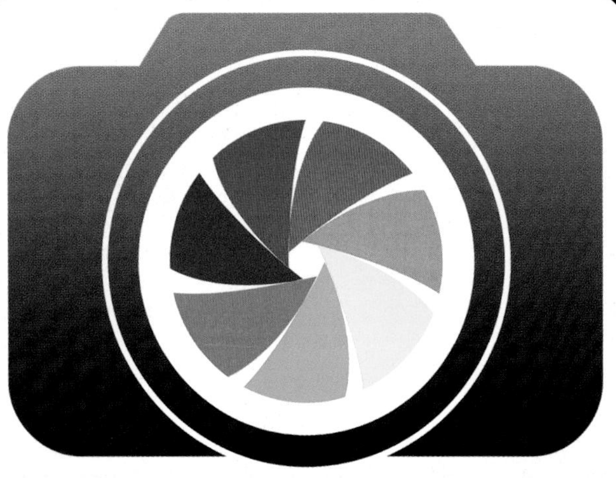

SNAPPED! BEST OF 2024!

Lethal weapon!

Forget about her tekkers, Ona Batlle could take an eye out with that ponytail!

Hero Haaland!

Where can we get ourselves one of those soft toys?

Bayern's bucking "ball"!

Leon Goretzka lasted about 30 seconds before falling off!

Job swap!

Does Martin Odegaard fancy a career change?

Funny fans!

THAT'S SUPER JOHN McGINN TO YOU!

These Villa supporters paid tribute to John McGinn!

The haka!

Elanga is hoping to get a call-up to New Zealand's rugby union side!

Shirt swap!

Trai Hume really wanted Anthony Gordon's jersey!

Worried Wood!

What has Chris Wood lost behind the billboard?

I CAN'T FIND MY PHONE!

Guess who?

We'll give you a clue... she's a goalkeeper!

Walker Fountain!

We've heard Kyle Walker is considering a light show too!

THAT WOULD BE TOP!

Don't try this at home!

We'd recommend disinfecting the ball first, Adingra!

THE NEXT BIG THING...

ADAM WHARTON

MATCH is here to tell you about the young stars that are getting ready to take over the global game...

WHO?

Adam Wharton, one of the fastest rising talents that MATCH has ever seen, who came out of absolutely nowhere to become a Prem star and England midfielder!

WHAT'S SO GOOD ABOUT HIM?

Wharton only made his Premier League debut in February 2024 after joining Crystal Palace from Championship side Blackburn, but instantly looked like he'd played there all his life! He's so calm on the ball, loves playing quick, crisp passes, hardly ever loses possession and loves getting stuck into tackles too!

DID YOU KNOW?

Adam's big brother Scott is also a pro footballer from Blackburn's academy – he still plays in Rovers' defence!

IN NUMBERS!

16 Premier League games that Wharton had played when he received his first England call-up for Euro 2024!

£18M Transfer fee that Crystal Palace paid to sign Wharton from Blackburn – that could prove to be an absolute bargain!

8 Goals and assists combined that Wharton bagged for both clubs across the 2023-24 season – not bad for a DM!

4 Crystal Palace players included in England's Euro 2024 squad – more than any other club!

WHO DOES HE PLAY LIKE?

English football has produced lots of exciting wingers and attacking midfielders in recent years, but there haven't been as many DMs that can help the team boss games with their passing. That's why there's so much buzz about Wharton – he could be England's deep-lying playmaker in the same way that Toni Kroos was for Germany!

WHAT DID HE DO IN 2024?

Even Wharton himself wouldn't have dreamt of making such a good start to life in the Prem! His arrival played a big part in Palace finishing the season so strongly, winning six of their last seven games with him in the side, and saw him earn his first England call-up. The midfielder was one of the shock call-ups for Gareth Southgate's Euro 2024 squad, and made his debut in the warm-up victory against Bosnia & Herzegovina!

WHAT'S NEXT?

After such an exciting start to life at the top, Wharton will be under pressure in 2025 – but if he can deal with it in the same way that he deals with any ball into his feet, he'll be fine! Palace signed him on a five-year deal, but that won't put off the Premier League big boys – we reckon he'll be playing Champo League football very soon!

MIDFIELD MAESTROS!

These young stars have the potential to boss the middle of the pitch for years to come...

FLORIAN WIRTZ
Bayer Leverkusen & Germany

Wirtz is already a massive star after shining in Leverkusen's unbeaten title win and for Germany at Euro 2024!

XAVI SIMONS
RB Leipzig & Netherlands

The CAM started in Barca's academy before PSG snapped him up! Since then he's had some epic loan spells at PSV and RB Leipzig!

JOAO NEVES
PSG & Portugal

Neves won the Portuguese league title at the age of 18 with Benfica in 2022-23, and sealed a mega-money move to PSG last summer!

OSCAR GLOUKH
Red Bull Salzburg & Israel

Keep an eye on the diminutive playmaker – he's going to be lighting up a bigger league than the Austrian Bundesliga very soon!

GAVI
Barcelona & Spain

It feels like Gavi has been bossing games for club and country for ages, so it's easy to forget that he's only just turned 20!

HARVEY ELLIOTT
Liverpool & England

The ex-Fulham wonderkid is set to play a big role in Arne Slot's new-look Liverpool – he's got an absolute wand of a left foot!

FOOTY'S BEST ACADEMIES!

MATCH checks out ten of the clubs with the best football academies in the world!

FACTFILE!

GOAT Academy Product: Steven Gerrard

Best Current Star: Trent Alexander-Arnold

One To Watch: Curtis Jones

Biggest Academy Sale: Raheem Sterling to Man. City ★ £49 million

LIVERPOOL

Liverpool legends Jamie Carragher, **Robbie Fowler**, Michael Owen and **Steven Gerrard** all came through their academy, while former gaffer Jurgen Klopp nurtured some proper exciting talents in recent years - not least Trent Alexander-Arnold! In 2023-24, the likes of Jarell Quansah, Conor Bradley, Jayden Danns and Bobby Clark all made their mark on the senior squad!

BARCELONA

Barcelona's La Masia academy is arguably the most famous on the planet! The boarding school teaches young talents to play in the club's unique style, with tiki-taka trained to perfection! They've produced the likes of **Leo Messi**, Gerard Pique, Xavi, **Andres Iniesta** and Sergio Busquets, while Gavi, Lamine Yamal and Pau Cubarsi are more recent graduates!

FACTFILE!

GOAT Academy Product: Lionel Messi

Best Current Star: Gavi

One To Watch: Pau Cubarsi

Biggest Academy Sale: Cesc Fabregas to Chelsea ★ £32 million

SIZZLING STARLETS!

MATCH checks out some of the Premier League's most exciting academy talents aged under 21!

ETHAN NWANERI
Arsenal

He became the youngest player to appear in the top flight of English football in 2022 at just 15 years old! Outstanding talent!

JAMIE DONLEY
Tottenham

The cultured left-footed baller can play as an attacking midfielder or up front and has incredible vision! 2025 could be his breakout year!

FACTFILE!

GOAT Academy Product: Bernardo Silva

Best Current Star: Antonio Silva

One To Watch: Joao Rego

Biggest Academy Sale: Joao Felix to Atletico Madrid ★ £113 million

BENFICA

No club has earned more profit from academy products over the past five years than the Portuguese giants, raking in more than £500 million on academy player sales alone! The club's aim is to have two starlets join the senior squad every season, with the likes of **Bernardo Silva**, Ruben Dias, Joao Cancelo, **Ederson** and Joao Felix all passing through over the past decade. Wow!

AJAX

It all started with legendary baller **Johan Cruyff**, whose Total Football principles have shaped the club ever since! As well as Cruyff, who their stadium is named after, the Eredivisie giants have produced some of the Netherlands' best-ever players, including **Dennis Bergkamp**, Edgar Davids, Patrick Kluivert, Clarence Seedorf and Wesley Sneijder!

FACTFILE!

GOAT Academy Product: Johan Cruyff

Best Current Star: Brian Brobbey

One To Watch: Jorrel Hato

Biggest Academy Sale: Matthijs de Ligt to Bayern Munich ★ £68 million

SANTOS

Fans in Brazil bicker over who has the best academy - Sao Paulo or Santos - but there's no denying Santos have produced the better players overall! As well as one of the game's GOATs in **Pele**, they also produced the country's all-time record scorer in **Neymar**. More recently, Rodrygo and Chelsea duo Angelo Gabriel and Deivid Washington have emerged!

FACTFILE!

GOAT Academy Product: Pele

Best Current Star: Ivonei

One To Watch: JP Chermont

Biggest Academy Sale: Neymar to Barcelona ★ £71.4 million

LEO CASTLEDINE

Chelsea

The midfielder made his senior debut as a substitute in Chelsea's EFL Cup semi-final win v Middlesbrough in January 2024!

KOBBIE MAINOO

Man. United

The box-to-box England midfielder was probably the biggest breakout star of 2023-24, keeping Casemiro out of United's XI!

FACTFILE!

GOAT Academy Product: Bobby Charlton

Best Current Star: Marcus Rashford

One To Watch: Kobbie Mainoo

Biggest Academy Sale: David Beckham to Real Madrid ★ £25 million

MAN. UNITED

It's not the juggernaut it once was in the Sir Alex Ferguson, Class of '92 era, but we can't feature the best academies without mentioning Carrington! An academy graduate has been named in United's squad for the past 85 years, including the likes of **Bobby Charlton**, George Best, **David Beckham**, Paul Scholes, Gary Neville and Marcus Rashford!

SPORTING

"Effort, Dedication, Devotion, Glory" are the first and last words the hopefuls see as they enter and leave Sporting's academy, which is named after **Cristiano Ronaldo**! As well as CR7, that mantra has helped produce the likes of Luis Figo, Nani, Rafael Leao, **Joao Moutinho**, Joao Palhinha and Nuno Mendes!

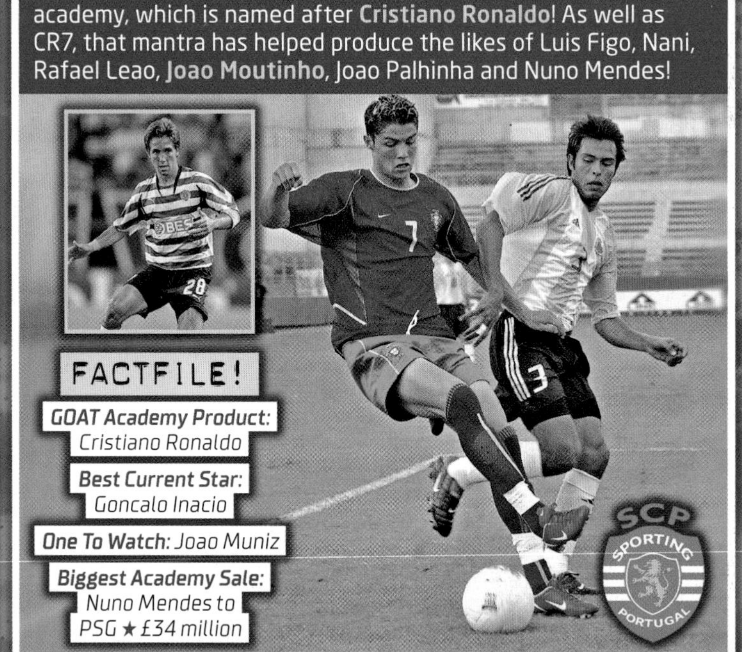

FACTFILE!

GOAT Academy Product: Cristiano Ronaldo

Best Current Star: Goncalo Inacio

One To Watch: Joao Muniz

Biggest Academy Sale: Nuno Mendes to PSG ★ £34 million

BAYERN MUNICH

The German giants have invested a lot of money into their academy over the years and they've reaped the rewards! Legends Philipp Lahm, **Franz Beckenbauer**, Thomas Muller, **Bastian Schweinsteiger** and Toni Kroos are just some of the names to have become football icons after breaking through at the club!

FACTFILE!

GOAT Academy Product: Franz Beckenbauer

Best Current Star: Thomas Muller

One To Watch: Aleksandar Pavlovic

Biggest Academy Sale: Toni Kroos to Real Madrid ★ £19.7 million

CONOR BRADLEY

Liverpool

The young Northern Ireland right-back stepped in brilliantly for Alexander-Arnold in 2023-24 and looks set to have a huge future at the club!

GEORGE EARTHY

West Ham

The midfielder joined West Ham's academy when he was six and has risen through the ranks, scoring his first senior goal last season. Class!

TOMMI O'REILLY

Aston Villa

The midfielder, who has captained Villa's Under-21s, made his senior debut in 2023 and has been compared to Phil Foden!

FACTFILE!

GOAT Academy Product:
John Terry

Best Current Star:
Reece James

One To Watch:
Dujuan Richards

Biggest Academy Sale:
Mason Mount to Man. United ★ £55 million

CHELSEA

Even though Chelsea have spent so much on young stars in recent years, their record at producing ballers is unquestionable – in fact, they've made more money on academy products than any English side in recent years! Some forgotten former academy gems include Michael Olise, Jamal Musiala, **Dominic Solanke**, Marc Guehi and Declan Rice!

FACTFILE!

GOAT Academy Product:
Alfredo Di Stefano

Best Current Star:
Santiago Simon

One To Watch:
Franco Mastantuono

Biggest Academy Sale:
Javier Saviola to Barcelona ★ £15 million

RIVER PLATE

Argentinian arch-rivals Boca Juniors and River Plate both boast mega impressive academies, and picking between the two is almost impossible! Even though Boca produced Diego Maradona, River's set-up has overtaken them recently, with the likes of **Julian Alvarez**, Enzo Fernandez and new Man. City star Claudio Echeverri all breaking through!

OSCAR BOBB
Man. City

The wicked Norway winger joined City's academy in 2019 when he was just 16 and made his big breakthrough in 2023-24. Baller!

FRASER HARPER
Wolves

The midfielder, who joined from Bristol City when he was just 13, was handed a first pro contract in 2023 when he turned 17!

EMMA HAYES'... CHELSEA

No manager has dominated the Women's Super League like EMMA HAYES – and it'll be a long time before anyone gets close to her record! We look back at her career as Chelsea Women's boss...

CHELSEA ARRIVAL

After beginning her coaching career in the United States, Hayes arrived at Chelsea during the 2012 season. Strange as it seems now, she spent her first two years battling at the bottom of the table, but she guided the team to safety!

JI JOINS

In 2014, Hayes made one of her most important signings – South Korea midfielder Ji So-yun. One of the WSL's best-ever foreign players, Ji kick-started the Hayes era by bagging the winner in the 2014-15 FA Cup final, the first of the manager's 16 trophies!

TITLE NO.1

With one trophy already in the bag for 2014-15, Hayes completed the double two months later by sealing the WSL crown! It was close, pipping Man. City by just two points, but five straight wins at the end of the season brought the title to West London!

INVINCIBLES

After losing the 2016 title to Man. City, Chelsea bounced back in style. They won the shorter 2017 Spring Series title, then just kept on winning, going the entire 2017-18 campaign unbeaten and then beating Arsenal in the FA Cup final to seal another double!

scrapbook!

CHAMPO LEAGUE SEMI-FINALISTS

After becoming England's dominant team, Chelsea started to compete in Europe. In both 2017-18 and 2018-19, The Blues made it to the Champions League semi-finals, but lost 5-2 to Wolfsburg and 3-2 to Lyon on aggregate respectively. Gutting!

BOUNCING BACK

The 2018-19 campaign was a tough year for Hayes as Chelsea went trophyless for the first time in two years. They were back on top in 2019-20, but there wasn't a lot to celebrate – the COVID pandemic interrupted the season in March, and The Blues were only handed the WSL title on a points-per-game average!

HERE COMES KERR

Australia superstar Sam Kerr arrived in January 2020, but didn't play much at first due to COVID. She proved she was worth every penny in 2020-21 though, bagging 31 goals as Chelsea sealed a domestic treble of WSL, FA Cup and League Cup trophies. Legends!

EUROPEAN FINALISTS

Chelsea's season would have been absolutely perfect – maybe even the best by any English team ever – if they'd won the 2020-21 CL trophy as well! But after beating German giants Wolfsburg and Bayern Munich, they got totally outclassed in the final, losing 4-0 to Barcelona!

INDIVIDUAL HONOURS

Hayes was rewarded for Chelsea's incredible 2020-21 season with two personal prizes. She became the first manager to go into the WSL Hall of Fame, and then was named the world's best women's manager at the 2021 FIFA Best Awards!

THREE IN A ROW

Since its formation in 2011, no team had ever won three WSL titles in a row before, and there were plenty of moments during 2021-22 when it looked like that wouldn't change. But with the help of some epic comebacks and dramatic late goals, Hayes' Chelsea won their last nine games to hold off Arsenal, winning the title by a point!

ANOTHER CUP TRIUMPH

A week after securing the WSL title, Chelsea were back at Wembley for another FA Cup final, this time v Man. City. They suffered a setback after conceding an 89th-minute equaliser, but Kerr was there to save them again, banging in the winner to make it 3-2 in extra-time!

LYON PENALTY DRAMA

Chelsea's quarter-final clash with Lyon in 2022-23 was one of the most dramatic CL games ever! When The Blues fell 2-1 behind on aggregate in extra-time it looked all over for them – until they equalised in the 128th minute and then won a penalty shootout!

MORE CL HEARTBREAK

The CL semi-finals saw Chelsea drawn against Barca once again. They hugely improved on their last meeting, and pushed the Spanish giants all the way, but went down 2-1 on aggregate! "The better team lost," Hayes said afterwards!

SAYING GOODBYE

Having won yet another WSL-FA Cup double in 2022-23, Chelsea started the 2023-24 season strongly. They went top in November with a 6-0 win against Aston Villa, but that's when Hayes dropped the bombshell that she would leave to join the USWNT at the end of the season!

BARCA BLUES

Hayes was desperate to sign off with CL glory – the one trophy she'd never won! Once again, she took her team to Barca in the semis, and The Blues pulled off a stunning result by winning 1-0 with an Erin Cuthbert goal – but their dreams were crushed by a 2-0 home defeat!

PERFECT SEND-OFF

European defeat meant Chelsea had to win the WSL to give Hayes her perfect send-off, and they trailed Man. City with two games to go. But Arsenal did her a huge favour by beating City with two late goals, and The Blues went top on the final day with an epic 6-0 win over Man. United!

BIG MATCH QUIZ!

How many of these tough WSL teasers can you get right?

You've got a 50/50 chance of getting these tricky Women's Super League questions right! Just tick the answer you think is correct...

1. Which lethal England forward scored more WSL goals in 2023-24?

LAUREN HEMP / LAUREN JAMES

2. Which Asian country does West Ham's Riko Ueki play for?

JAPAN / SOUTH KOREA

3. Which WSL wonderkid is younger?

KAROLINE OLESEN / MISSY GOODWIN

4. Which club finished higher in the WSL table in 2023-24?

TOTTENHAM / LIVERPOOL

5. Which mega rival has more all-time Women's Super League trophies?

MAN. CITY / MAN. UNITED

6. Which quality boot brand does Arsenal striker Alessia Russo wear?

ADIDAS / NIKE

STAT ATTACK!

Which player does this stat refer to?

IN NOVEMBER 2023, SHE BECAME JUST THE SECOND PLAYER TO REACH 100 WSL GOALS AND ASSISTS COMBINED!

A. Nikita Parris

B. Sam Kerr

C. Beth Mead

LIST IT!

Put two minutes on a timer and write down ten Women's Championship clubs!

☐ ____________________
☐ ____________________
☐ ____________________
☐ ____________________
☐ ____________________
☐ ____________________
☐ ____________________
☐ ____________________
☐ ____________________
☐ ____________________

ODD ONE OUT!

VIVIANE ASSEYI

PAULINE BREMER

GURO REITEN

JILL ROORD

Which of these Women's Super League stars has never played in Germany's Frauen-Bundesliga?

WORDSEARCH

Find 30 WSL stars to score at least three goals in 2023-24 in this massive grid!

- Asseyi
- Beever-Jones
- Blackstenius
- Cayman
- Clinton
- Cuthbert
- Daly
- Foord
- Garcia
- Haug
- Hemp
- Hobinger
- Idhusoy
- James
- Kelly
- Kerr
- Leon
- Malard
- Mead
- Nusken
- Parris
- Petermann
- Rantala
- Roord
- Russo
- Shaw
- Terland
- Thestrup
- Thomas
- Williams

N D G B I Q Y K L H N O D O C V L B Y I L E I X V Y D H V C Q O
C U U Q D Y P M Z E K G C V Y O O F N V C L I N T O N P Q D Y Y
X W T R M T X R H B E T M O S W M U K A Z H J G M C K P Y I K P
I S G H Q G E J Y M A Q W V S R T P R U S S O O W C N D Y X C P
N J J B O I D O X S A U A H F U M X B A Y V J T Q Y R U V P O Z
K M H Z G M H I N O X O B Y U M E G L A B X F Y M A R L Y V D E
M W M E D U A R E Z U K Y P M T Y J L C E K Z B L C W Z K W J S
T H W C D H G S W C J C U C R K S U I K S C S A E R X V G G D O
Y H W N B P L T R T N G N Q K V B X N W V T M M J R K G X R R B
S P U O N B V J M A I V P Q L C G Y U F T D M W Z B M S A T G E
J U Q U U H F R U T N O U Q X Z M W D A B M W Q B P E F G A A R
G V Z J U R E O C X I T N Q W L E O N Q J A R N U S K E N G R Y
P T G Q P T F M O Z Y I A E D F X N B Q H I V H W W T U I H C K
U Z P R P Y Z U P R E Z I L H P V K S S W P A R R I S W N M I P
T P T O G A Q S C O D V F A A Q P R U P F P Y Y L G N A L I A Y
S Q S B A I Y J C A J R H J E V C L T W M W K U C L L B V J G B
O B R O O R D T R S H R S I X U Q D D I C J E D A L Y N R F A Q
T L P E E F K O E S O U L A P H L M E A D I R V T X O T A S Z U
Z R L M Z E W C F E B T E H G G Q T N N A X R U O K Z M N W M W
A Z S D I E R K V Y I T B G B N I T G B V I N Y R G E W Z B S A
V R P H M R Q K O I N U L E Q G Q T U W A H O S N Z V C E V H F
K V R T Z R F W S Z G K J V E T Q V X Z T S T N C U T H B E R T
S I M N F B V C S S E A S A F V X N F Y U P A V H D M Y B R G A
T B T E J B T Y I G R J K J A F E C P H H M K V J I H L V R X H
F Q N S N T Y C T F S F E C V R U R D L R T W A I H A W W W D I
E K G G E B T H T X A O L P O S K I J E B C K H O V U I P T A G
U T M L R Z Q T X G J A L J A M E S T O D M R A P A G J C H A X
A V F L U K N I E X T O Y H E U W E U N N R L I W F M F F E W J
T Z T C I A Y Y Y R Y O M D I V P D W U N E S H Q H E O F S K U
F P W U M Y F V A A L E J G Y L W W W B Z A S M U N P P S T H M
R H O Y C K F S C C J A S W I L L I A M S L P B M V S F R R I R
F X A K M W H P X V F L N Q M Q E D M R M X S Z D G I G A U C Y
N C H Z H V J W S F O A P D L A X M O G Y R G A T O Z Z M P K G
V Z K J V Z S T E Z B L A C K S T E N I U S E E O X W N L F D L

ANSWERS ON PAGE 94

adidas PREDATORS... THROUGH THE YEARS!

In 2024, the PREDATOR celebrated 30 years since its first launch in 1994! We open the archive to present some of the coolest Preds to have dropped during that period...

Predator X
2009
Predator AdiPower
2011
Predator
Lethal Zones
2012
Predator
Lethal
Zones II
2013
Predator Instinct
2014
Predator Touch
2016
Predator 18
2018
Predator 19
2019
Predator
Mutator
2020
Predator Freak
2021
Predator Edge
2022
Predator
Accuracy
2023

DESIGN YOUR OWN PREDS!

Now you've seen some of our fave adidas Predators through the years, we want you to design a new pair for the future!

TOP TIPS!

Make sure you get the iconic adidas three stripes on the boots somewhere!

We want you to be creative – try to use other boots for inspiration rather than just copying them!

We don't mind if you want to have an outrageous design or prefer to keep it simple!

If it helps, write down some bullet points to help explain your ultra-cool design!

We'll post out fave ones on social media and feature the best in the magazine!

SEND IT IN!

Send us a photo of your drawing and we'll feature the best ones in MATCH magazine and on our epic social media channels!

Email: match.magazine@kelsey.co.uk
facebook.com/matchmagazine
X.com/matchmagazine
instagram.com/matchmagofficial

Football's Biggest WHAT IFS?

MATCH looks back at the moments that could've changed footy forever...

WHAT IF... Harry Kane played for Arsenal?

Although he's Tottenham's record scorer and a club legend, Kane's football journey actually began across North London with Arsenal's Under-8s! The Gunners released him before he turned ten, but imagine if they'd kept faith with him! The England skipper might be Arsenal's all-time top scorer instead of Spurs, and he might have led them to a title or two in the last ten years!

WHAT IF... Celtic & Rangers played in England?

Over the years, people have argued that Celtic and Rangers have outgrown Scottish football and that they should play in the English Premier League instead! The atmospheres at the Glasgow grounds when the likes of Liverpool and Man. United were in town would be electric, and with the PL riches in their banks, we reckon the Old Firm duo would be serious contenders!

WHAT IF... Musiala & Haaland played for England?

England have lots of great attackers, but they could have had even more! As a youngster, Germany wonderkid Jamal Musiala won 19 caps for England's youth teams, while Erling Haaland was eligible for The Three Lions too! The striker was born in Leeds, but ultimately played for Norway just like his dad, Alfie!

WHAT IF... Barcelona signed Cristiano Ronaldo?

Back in 2003, Barcelona had the chance to sign Cristiano Ronaldo from Sporting - but they signed his club-mate Ricardo Quaresma instead, and CR7 joined Man. United! Barcelona still won loads without the Portuguese legend, but if they'd had CR7 and Leo Messi in the same team, they'd have been absolutely unstoppable!

WHAT IF... Man. City's owners bought Everton?

Man. City have been totally dominant in recent years, becoming the first English team to ever win four titles in a row, while Everton have spent the last couple of seasons battling relegation - but it could have been the other way around! Originally, Sheikh Mansour made an offer to buy The Toffees, but when it was rejected, he bought City instead and turned them into a winning machine!

FOOTY HAIRCUTS!

MATCH looks back on some of the wildest footy trims from over the years! Do you rate them or slate them?

1960s & '70s

MARTIN PETERS
WEST HAM

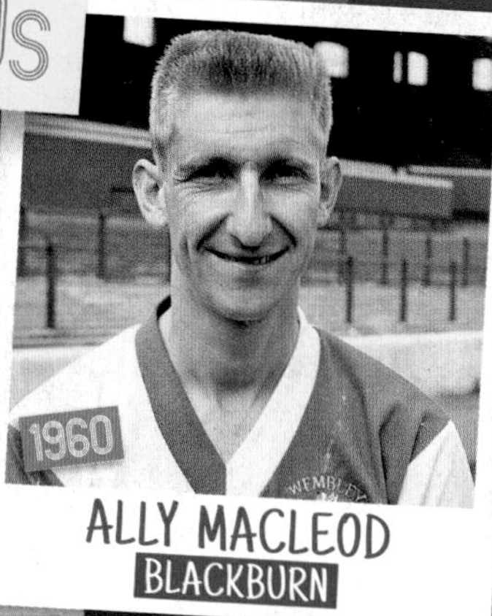

ALLY MACLEOD
BLACKBURN

RON ATKINSON
CAMBRIDGE UNITED

BOBBY CHARLTON
MAN. UNITED

NOEL BROTHERSTON
TOTTENHAM

TREVOR FRANCIS
BIRMINGHAM

CHARLIE GEORGE
ARSENAL

1971

GEORGE BEST
MAN. UNITED

1973

KEVIN KEEGAN
ENGLAND

GERRY GOW
BRISTOL CITY

TONY CURRIE
SHEFFIELD UNITED

GERRY FRANCIS
QPR

1979

MIKE FLANAGAN
CRYSTAL PALACE

1980s & '90s

BRYAN ROBSON
MAN. UNITED

TOMMY CATON
ARSENAL

ALAN BRAZIL
MAN. UNITED

ALAN BILEY
RANGERS

CHARLIE NICHOLAS
ARSENAL

TARIBO WEST
NIGERIA

HENRIK LARSSON
SWEDEN

1998

DAN PETRESCU
ROMANIA

TONY DALEY
ASTON VILLA

CARLOS VALDERRAMA
COLOMBIA

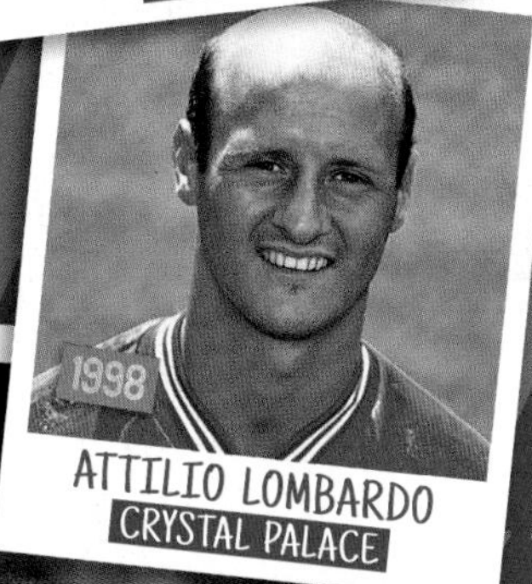

ATTILIO LOMBARDO
CRYSTAL PALACE

BARRY VENISON
NEWCASTLE

ALEXI LALAS
USA

RENE HIGUITA
COLOMBIA

TURN OVER FOR MORE HAIRCUTS!

2000s

DAVID SEAMAN
ARSENAL

RONALDO
BRAZIL

ABEL XAVIER
MIDDLESBROUGH

FREDDIE LJUNGBERG
ARSENAL

DAVID BECKHAM
ENGLAND

JOE COLE
ENGLAND

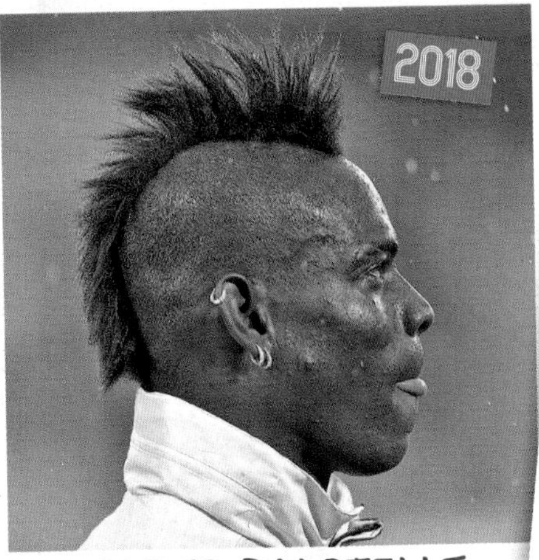

MARIO BALOTELLI
NICE

BACARY SAGNA
AUXERRE

RAUL MEIRELES
PORTUGAL

MAMADOU SAKHO
FRANCE

MAROUANE FELLAINI
MAN. UNITED

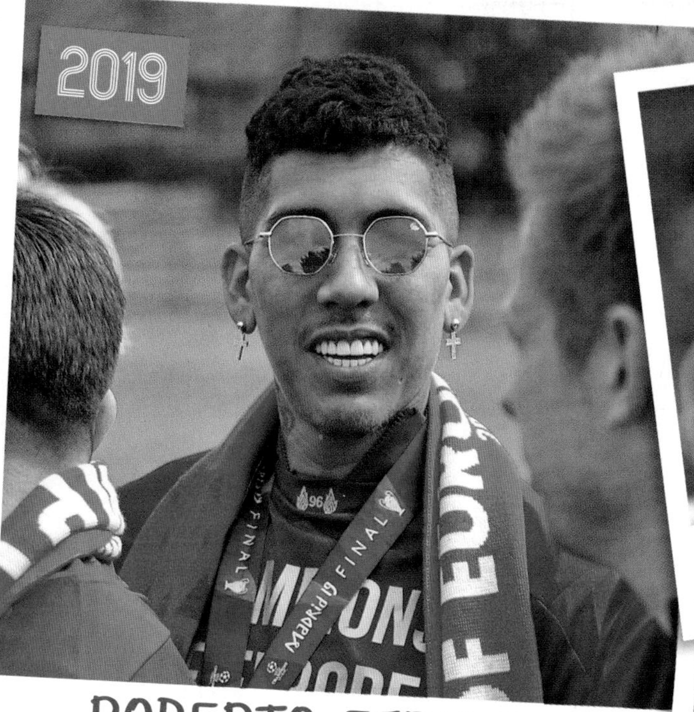

ROBERTO FIRMINO
LIVERPOOL

MAREK HAMSIK
SLOVAKIA

FABRICIO COLOCCINI
SAN LORENZO

DJIBRIL CISSE
QPR

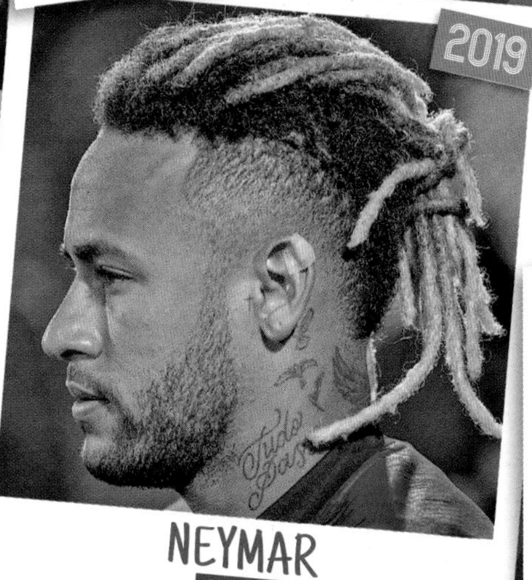

NEYMAR
PSG

KYLIAN MBAPPE
PSG

STEPHAN EL SHAARAWY
ITALY

PAUL POGBA
MAN. UNITED

BENOIT ASSOU-EKOTTO
TOTTENHAM

GERVINHO
ARSENAL

ALEJANDRO GARNACHO
MAN. UNITED

ANTOINE GRIEZMANN
ATLETICO MADRID

THE NEXT BIG THING...

ENDRICK

MATCH is here to tell you about the young stars that are getting ready to take over the global game...

WHO?

Endrick, the wicked wonderkid who's just joined Real Madrid after tearing up Brazilian football as a teenager!

WHAT'S SO GOOD ABOUT HIM?

Brazil fans haven't been this excited about a young player since Neymar first burst onto the scene in the early 2010s! Endrick has starred at one of the biggest clubs in Brazil, Palmeiras, since the age of 16, helping them win two league titles and then reach the semi-finals of the Copa Libertadores - South America's version of the Champions League!

DID YOU KNOW?

Endrick visited Chelsea's Cobham training ground with his parents in 2022, and was rumoured to be keen on a move to The Blues, before Real Madrid stepped in!

IN NUMBERS!

165 Number of goals that Endrick scored in just 169 games for Palmeiras' youth teams!

16 Age of Endrick when he bagged his first league goal for Palmeiras to become the second-youngest goalscorer in Brazilian top-flight history!

17 Endrick's age when he scored against England in March 2024 to become the youngest male goalscorer in Wembley history. Wow!

11 Goals that Endrick scored on the way to winning the 2023 Brazilian league title – nobody bagged more for Palmeiras!

WHO DOES HE PLAY LIKE?

Brazil have always produced top talent, and in recent years they've had loads of sick ballers like Vinicius Junior, Neymar and Rodrygo, but it's been ages since they had a world-class No.9! That's why everybody in Brazil is so excited about Endrick – with his combination of top technical talent, physicality and goalscoring, he plays like their legendary striker Ronaldo!

WHAT DID HE DO IN 2024?

Every big club in the world wanted Endrick, but Real Madrid moved quickest to sign him in a deal worth over £50m! That was in 2022, but Brazilian players can't move to Europe until they turn 18, so he had to wait until his birthday in July 2024 to arrive in Spain. While he was waiting, he scored his first international goal, bagging at Wembley in a 1-0 win over England!

WHAT'S NEXT?

Like Brazil, Real Madrid also have space in their attack for a new No.9! The Spanish giants have a squad packed with attacking talent, including Kylian Mbappe, Vinicius, Rodrygo and Jude Bellingham, so don't expect Endrick to dominate the Bernabeu in his first season, but he'll be leading the attack for club and country for years to come!

S. AMERICAN STARLETS!

South America never stops producing huge talents! Check out these wicked wonderkids...

SAVINHO
Man. City & Brazil

City signed the winger from partner club Troyes after he bossed La Liga in 2023-24 on loan at Girona, bagging nine goals and ten assists!

MATIAS SOULE
Roma & Argentina

The 21-year-old attacking midfielder shone on loan at Frosinone in 2023-24 – now he's ready to star for Roma after joining from Juve!

KENDRY PAEZ
Independiente del Valle & Ecuador

The 17-year-old is already a star for his country! Keep an eye out for him in 2025 – he'll join Chelsea when he turns 18 in May!

ESTEVAO WILLIAN
Palmeiras & Brazil

Another star from Palmeiras' academy, and another wicked wonderkid who'll join Chelsea when he turns 18 in the summer of 2025!

CLAUDIO ECHEVERRI
River Plate & Argentina

Joining Man. City in January 2025, the gem starred in River Plate's league title win and shone at the Under-17 World Cup for Argentina!

VITOR ROQUE
Real Betis & Brazil

The on-loan ace fired Athletico Paranaense to the Libertadores final and Brazil to the South America U20 Championship to earn his move to Europe!

BEST MOMENTS

Was Euro 2024 the craziest football tournament of all time?

GREAT GOALS!

XHERDAN SHAQIRI

The Swiss star's first-time curler against Scotland was a real screamer, although he gets nil points for his failed knee-slide celebration. LOL!

NICOLAE STANCIU

The Romania midfielder's first-time long-range strike against Ukraine was even more impressive because the ball was bobbling as it arrived at his feet!

JUDE BELLINGHAM

Talk about a Euros clutch moment, the England ace scored an overhead kick when The Three Lions were on the brink of a shock exit to Slovakia!

ARDA GULER & MERT MULDER

There was a 2-for-1 offer on worldies in the Turkey v Georgia match - Mert Muldur's amazing volley and Arda Guler's "golazo" from long range. Wow!

RECORD BREAKERS!

YOUNG GUNS!

Lamine Yamal became the Euros' youngest player, assist maker and scorer, while Arda Guler became the youngest to net on his Euros debut!

GOLDEN OLDIES!

Portugal's Pepe became the oldest player to feature at the Euros at 41 years old, while Luka Modric became the tourno's oldest scorer at 38!

EARLY AND LATE!

Nedim Bajrami scored the fastest-ever Euros goal after just 23 seconds, while Kevin Csoboth's 100th-minute goal was the latest ever scored!

RONALDO RECORDS!

Cristiano Ronaldo became the first player to feature in six European Championships and the competition's all-time top assister. Total legend!

OF EURO 2024!

MATCH looks back at the pick of last summer's epic action!

CRAZY CELEBRATIONS!

GEORGES MIKAUTADZE

We didn't need our binoculars to notice the Georgia striker, because he made sure he was spotted with his wicked performances for the underdogs!

DAN NDOYE

As the saying goes, you should never wake a sleeping Ndoye – or should that be lion? The mega pacy wideman was a roaring success all tourno for his side!

FRANCISCO CONCEICAO

We're sure the Portugal young gun would say this was worth the yellow card after he came off the bench to score a last-gasp winner v Czech Republic!

LAMINE YAMAL & NICO WILLIAMS

Spain's wonderkid wingers Yamal and Williams were the bromance of the summer – their LOL dancing celebration in the 4-1 win over Georgia was class!

HAIRY SITUATION!

YANNICK CARRASCO

BELGIUM

ANDREI RATIU

ROMANIA

BARIS ALPER YILMAZ

TURKEY

ROBERT ANDRICH

GERMANY

MEGA MATCHES!

BELGIUM 0-1 SLOVAKIA

Slovakia stunned a Belgium side 45 places above them in the rankings in a chaotic group-stage match!

TURKEY 3-1 GEORGIA

An epic atmosphere, two worldies and a goal scored in injury time after the goalkeeper went up for a corner...

NETHERLANDS 2-3 AUSTRIA

This five-goal thriller eventually settled Group D, with Austria going ahead on three different occasions!

GEORGIA 2-0 PORTUGAL

Khvicha Kvaratskhelia's goal after just two minutes and Mikautadze's penalty sealed a Euros shock for the ages!

SUPER SUBS!

BREEL EMBOLO
After being introduced in the 74th minute against Hungary, Embolo clinched three points for the Swiss with a lovely lobbed finish over Peter Gulacsi in stoppage time!

OLLIE WATKINS
The Aston Villa striker sent England fans wild after coming off the bench in the semi-final v Netherlands and smashing a pinpoint winner into the bottom corner!

WOUT WEGHORST
Former Man. United target man Weghorst swept in a late winner two minutes after coming on to seal three points v Poland!

MATTIA ZACCAGNI
The jaw-dropping limbs after super sub Mattia Zaccagni's late equaliser for Italy against Croatia in the groups was like they'd won the final!

KLAUS GJASULA
Gjasula became the first substitute in Euros history to score both an own goal and a goal in the same match, with his 95th-minute finish earning Albania a draw against Croatia!

MIKEL MERINO
Merino's thumping 119th-minute header sent Spain into the semi-finals and eliminated hosts Germany! We loved his corner-flag dance too, which was a recreation of his dad's celebration at the same stadium 33 years earlier!

LUKAKU'S BAD LUCK!

v SLOVAKIA
VAR... OFFSIDE!

v SLOVAKIA
VAR... HANDBALL!

v ROMANIA
VAR... OFFSIDE!

WOW MOMENTS!

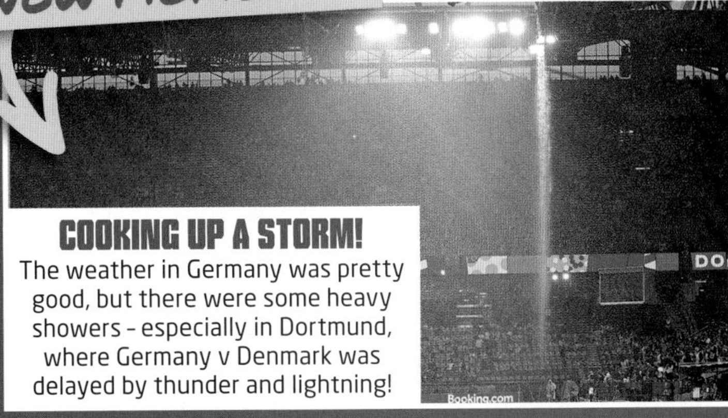

COOKING UP A STORM!

The weather in Germany was pretty good, but there were some heavy showers – especially in Dortmund, where Germany v Denmark was delayed by thunder and lightning!

THE DUTCH MARCH!

The Netherlands fans' march to the stadium for each game had MATCH in awe every single time! The streets were lined with orange everywhere!

MBAPPE'S MASK!

We're sure Kylian Mbappe would have preferred NOT to have broken his nose, but his mask was one of the iconic images of the Euros – especially when he took it off to celebrate a goal!

EPIC SAVE!

Turkey made it through to the quarter-finals thanks to a jaw-dropping last-minute save from goalkeeper Mert Gunok! He somehow tipped it past the post after a bouncing Austria header!

CZECH'S RED MIST!

Czech Republic exited the tournament with two red cards – for Antonin Barak after just 20 minutes and Tomas Chory after the final whistle – while Turkey got 11 yellow cards! The clash set a record for the most cards (18) in a single Euros fixture. Bonkers!

DANISH DELIGHT!

We all remember the sad scenes involving Christian Eriksen from Euro 2020, so to see him score versus Slovenia was one of the most uplifting moments from the Euros. Hero!

CRAZY FANS!

The fans were a reason Euro 2024 was such a big success! We spotted some proper LOL costumes!

PORTUGAL

SPAIN

DENMARK

ALBANIA

BELGIUM

SWITZERLAND

ROMANIA

FRANCE

ITALY

OWN GOALS!

Euro 2024 was one own goal short of the all-time record for the most "oggies" at a single European Championship! Here was a handful of them...

ANTONIO RUDIGER
v SCOTLAND

SAMET AKAYDIN
v PORTUGAL

MAX WOBER
v FRANCE

DONYELL MALEN
v AUSTRIA

JAN VERTONGHEN
v FRANCE

KEEPER KING!

In their last-16 clash against Slovenia, Portugal's Diogo Costa became the first goalkeeper to save three penalties in a Euros penalty shootout and the first to concede zero goals in a single Euros shootout!

PENALTY SAVE #1
v JOSIP ILICIC

PENALTY SAVE #2
v JURE BALKOVEC

PENALTY SAVE #3
v BENJAMIN VERBIC

STUNNING SPAIN!

STAR MAN!

Even though he had to go off injured at half-time in the final versus England, midfield magician Rodri had already done enough to be crowned the Player of the Tournament!

TOP SCORER!

Dani Olmo only played 31 minutes of Spain's first two games, but became a key main after Pedri's injury versus Germany and was the tourno's joint-top scorer on three goals!

TEEN TALENT!

Lamine Yamal created more chances than any other player, scored an epic long-range worldy v France, got an assist in the final and was crowned the Young Player of the Tournament!

EURO 2024 CHAMPS!

Spain were the best team in the tournament by miles! They won all their group games and beat Georgia, Germany, France and England en route to the trophy, without needing a single penalty shootout!

THE GAFFER!

Luis de la Fuente became the first coach to win the European Championship with three different age groups: the 2015 Under-19 Euros, the 2019 Under-21 Euros and Euro 2024!

SPAIN v THE WORLD!

Since the 2002 Champions League final, Spanish sides and the Spain national team have played in 23 major finals v non-Spanish teams and won the trophy on all 23 occasions. Mad!

ROCKING RECORDS!

Spain overtook Germany as the nation with the most Euros titles (4), and beat the record for the most goals scored by a team in a single tournament (15)!

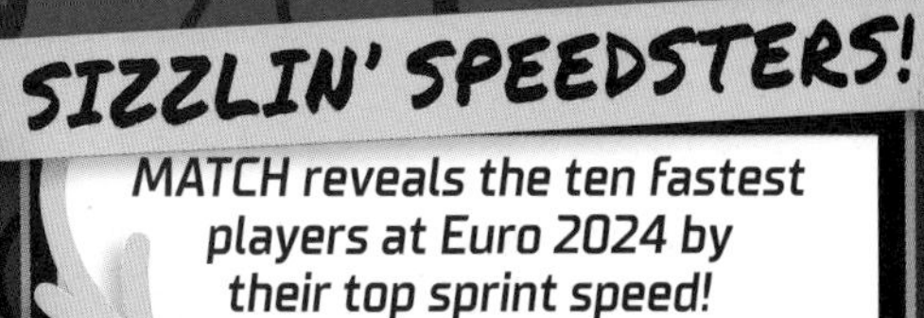

SIZZLIN' SPEEDSTERS!

MATCH reveals the ten fastest players at Euro 2024 by their top sprint speed!

1

KYLIAN MBAPPE
FRANCE
36.5km/h

2

FERRAN TORRES
SPAIN
36km/h

3

BENJAMIN SESKO
SLOVENIA
35.9km/h

4=

LEROY SANE
GERMANY
35.8km/h

4=

VALENTIN MIHAILA
ROMANIA
35.8km/h

6

THEO HERNANDEZ
FRANCE
35.7km/h

7=

DAN NDOYE
SWITZERLAND
35.6km/h

7=

MICKY VAN DE VEN
NETHERLANDS
35.6km/h

9

RASMUS HOJLUND
DENMARK
35.5km/h

10

RAFAEL LEAO
PORTUGAL
35.4km/h

CONTINENTAL

2024 didn't just see Spain crowned champions of Europe – there were also tournaments in Asia, Africa, Oceania and North and South America! We take a look at the other kings of the continents...

ASIAN CUP

Hosts: Qatar

Winners: Qatar ★ **Runners-up:** Jordan

Golden Boot: Akram Afif (Qatar), 8 goals

The story: Qatar stunk the place out when they hosted the 2022 World Cup, finishing rock bottom of their group after losing every game and scoring just once, but they're the kings of their continent after winning their second Asian Cup in a row! Wicked winger Akram Afif was the star, bagging a hat-trick in the final against underdogs Jordan, who shocked everyone by finishing second!

Argentina became the outright most successful nation in Copa America history, overtaking Uruguay with 16 all-time trophies!

Akram Afif

Akram Afif became just the third player to hit eight goals or more in a single edition of the Asian Cup after Iran's Ali Daei (1996) and Qatar's Almoez Ali (2019)!

COPA AMERICA

Hosts: United States

Winners: Argentina ★ **Runners-up:** Colombia

Golden Boot: Lautaro Martinez (Argentina), 5 goals

The story: The Copa America is usually a competition for South America, but this time it went north to the United States to help prepare for the 2026 World Cup. The hosts took part along with Canada, Mexico, Jamaica, Panama and Costa Rica, plus the ten South American teams. Reigning champions Argentina lifted back-to-back trophies for the first time since 1993, beating Colombia 1-0 in the final after extra-time thanks to Lautaro Martinez's goal!

Lautaro Martinez

OFC NATIONS CUP

Hosts: Vanuatu & Fiji

Winners: New Zealand ★ **Runners-up:** Vanuatu

Golden Boot: Roy Krishna (Fiji), 5 goals

The story: Football in Oceania is totally different to the rest of the world, as many of the players are amateur and just being able to take part in a major international tournament is a success! New Zealand usually dominate, and it was no different in 2024 as the All Whites swept to the trophy in impressive form. They beat co-hosts Vanuatu – appearing in their first-ever final – 3-0 in the showpiece!

Roy Krishna

Ivory Coast became the first host nation to win the Africa Cup of Nations in 18 years!

Emilio Nsue

New Zealand scored 15 times en route to the OFC Nations Cup trophy and didn't let in a single goal!

AFCON

Hosts: Ivory Coast

Winners: Ivory Coast ★ **Runners-up:** Nigeria

Golden Boot: Emilio Nsue (Equatorial Guinea), 5 goals

The story: The latest Africa Cup of Nations was one of the best roller-coaster rides we've ever been on! Hosts Ivory Coast sacked their manager after a 4-0 loss in the group stage, but somehow made it all the way to the final thanks to some dramatic late goals, then saw off Nigeria with a brilliant finish from ex-West Ham striker Sebastien Haller!

WHO'S YOUR MLS TEAM?

Wassup, dudes! Let's see which Major League Soccer side you should be following...

1

WHICH DIVISION?

Do you want your MLS team to be playing in the Eastern or Western Conference?

- If Eastern, go to question 2!
- If Western, go to question 4!

2

AMERICAN OR CANADIAN?

Do you want your club to be American or Canadian?

- If American, go to question 3!
- If Canadian, go to question 7!

3

MLS CUP CHAMPS?

Does your club need to have lifted the MLS Cup at least twice?

- If Yes, go to question 5!
- If No, go to question 8!

4

HOLLYWOOD-BASED?

Do you want your team to be based near Hollywood?

- If Yes, go to question 9!
- If No, go to question 6!

5

CAPITAL CLUB?

Do you want your team to be based in USA's capital city?

- If Yes, you should support D.C. United!
- If No, you should support Columbus Crew!

6

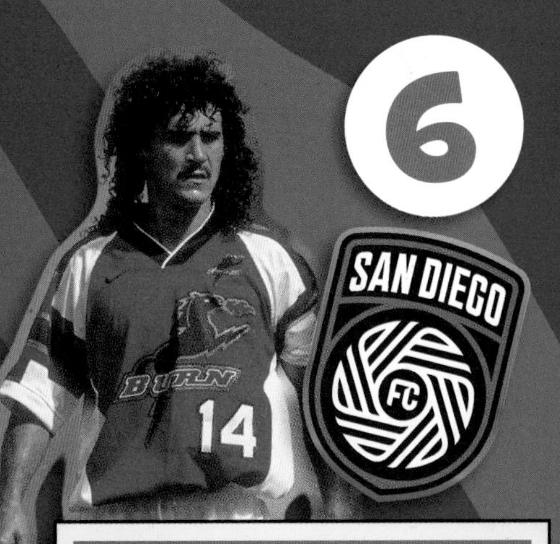

OLD OR NEW FRANCHISE?

Do you want your team to be one of the league's oldest or newest?

- If oldest, you should support FC Dallas!
- If newest, you should support San Diego FC!

7

RED OR BLUE?

Do you prefer your team to wear red or blue shirts?

- If Red, you should support Toronto FC!
- If Blue, you should support CF Montreal!

8

STADIUM SHARERS?

Do you want your club to share a stadium with an NFL team?

- If Yes, you should support New England Revolution!
- If No, go to question 10!

9

TOP TRANSFERS?

Do you want your club to be linked with Galactico signings?

- If Yes, you should support LA Galaxy!
- If No, you should support Los Angeles FC!

10

MESSI MANIA!

Do you think Lionel Messi is football's GOAT?

- If Yes, you should support Inter Miami!
- If No, you should support Nashville SC!

BENJAMIN SESKO

MATCH is here to tell you about the young stars that are getting ready to take over the global game...

WHO?

You might have seen Sesko in action for Slovenia at Euro 2024 – he led his country's attack, including in the group stage v England, after an impressive first season in the Bundesliga at RB Leipzig!

DID YOU KNOW?

As a kid, Sesko was a highly-rated basketball player that dreamed of playing professionally and he still shoots hoops and watches NBA now!

WHAT'S SO GOOD ABOUT HIM?

Sesko is a complete forward. He's tall, quick and strong, can finish with either foot and has the top class tekkerz to hold onto the ball even when he's surrounded by defenders! Most importantly, he's a proper goalscorer – the 21-year-old is already close to 100 career goals for FC Liefering, Red Bull Salzburg, RB Leipzig and Slovenia!

IN NUMBERS!

3 Austrian league titles that Sesko won during his time with Red Bull Salzburg!

18 Age of Sesko when he scored against Malta to become Slovenia's youngest-ever goalscorer, just months after becoming their youngest player!

5 Goals scored by Sesko in qualifying for Euro 2024 – the country's first major tournament since 2010, and their first Euros since 2000!

7 Consecutive Bundesliga games that Sesko scored in at the end of the 2023-24 season!

WHO DOES HE PLAY LIKE?

As a big and powerful front man that used to play for Red Bull Salzburg, the comparisons to Erling Haaland are obvious - but you won't see the big Norwegian popping stepovers and playing in his team-mates with slick flicks in the way Sesko does! The Slovenian has got way more technical ability, so we'd say he's more like a young Zlatan Ibrahimovic!

WHAT DID HE DO IN 2024?

RB Leipzig eased Sesko in slowly after signing him from Salzburg, but his form exploded after Christmas, smashing home 11 Bundesliga goals in the second half of the season! His form helped secure CL football for Leipzig, and ensured that he went to the Euros - where he guided his nation to the knockout stages for the first time ever - as one of the finals' most exciting young talents!

WHAT'S NEXT?

Sesko is one of the most wanted young strikers on the planet, but he committed his future to RB Leipzig by signing a new deal until 2029. But that doesn't mean he'll be at the club forever - we reckon he could be set for a big move in 2025 after he's scored even more goals in the Bundesliga and made an impact in the Champions League!

FEARSOME FORWARDS!

These attacking talents will also be banging in plenty of goals in the future! Check them out...

PARIS BRUNNER
Cercle Brugge & Germany

He joined Monaco from Borussia Dortmund and was loaned to Cercle Brugge for the 2024-25 season. He lifted up the U17 World Cup in 2023, scoring five!

EVAN FERGUSON
Brighton & Republic of Ireland

Ferguson is already a top talent - and he's only going to get better! He's one of only four players to hit a Prem hat-trick aged 18 or younger!

KENAN YILDIZ
Juventus & Turkey

Juve pulled off a great deal by signing Yildiz from Bayern Munich's academy - the 19-year old forward has already made a big impact at the Italian giants!

ALEJANDRO GARNACHO
Man. United & Argentina

Garnacho showed his world-class quality by scoring the Premier League Goal of the Season in 2023-24 with his mind-blowing bicycle kick v Everton!

JOHAN BAKAYAKO
PSV & Belgium

After coming through their top academy, Bakayoko helped PSV win the Dutch title in 2023-24 - but don't be surprised to see him in the Prem soon!

MAXIMILIAN BEIER
Borussia Dortmund & Germany

The target man fired Hoffenheim to Europa League footy by scoring 16 league goals in 2023-24, then went to Euro 2024 before joining Dortmund!

WORST PREM SEASONS... EVER!

Sheffield United wrote themselves into the history books last season, as they endured one of the top five worst-ever Premier League campaigns! Check out these sorry seasons...

DERBY

SEASON	POINTS	GOAL DIFFERENCE
2007-08	11	-69

The Rams are owners of a record they won't want to shout about...their measly 11 points in 2007-08, which included just one win all campaign, is actually the worst single-season points tally in the history of Europe's top five leagues! They also hold the unwanted Prem record for the most defeats in a single season (29) and the fewest goals scored (20). Ouch!

SUNDERLAND

SEASON	POINTS	GOAL DIFFERENCE
2005-06	15	-43

Before Sheffield United's disastrous 2023-24 campaign, The Black Cats appeared twice in the Prem's top five worst-ever seasons - with 2005-06 just trumping their failure of 2002-03! Upon their return to the top tier in 2005, they lost their first five games to extend a record losing streak to 20 games. They picked up seven points at home all season, another PL record!

SHEFFIELD UNITED

SEASON	POINTS	GOAL DIFFERENCE
2023-24	16	-69

Last season, The Blades became the first side in Premier League history to concede 100 goals in a single 38-game campaign! They let in at least one goal in all of their 19 away games, and shipped a record 13 goals to Newcastle - the most one team has conceded against another in a single season in the competition's history!

HUDDERSFIELD

SEASON	POINTS	GOAL DIFFERENCE
2018-19	16	-54

After escaping relegation in their debut season in the Premier League in 2017-18, all eyes were on Huddersfield to see if they could survive the second season curse! Spoiler alert...they couldn't! Weirdly, six of their 16 points came against Wolves, but that wasn't enough and they were relegated as early as March. Ouch!

ASTON VILLA

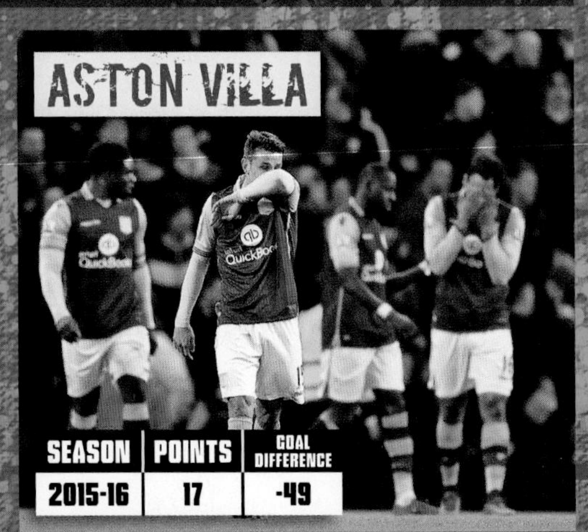

SEASON	POINTS	GOAL DIFFERENCE
2015-16	17	-49

The Villans may be a Champions League club now, but it was less than a decade ago when they were relegated from the Premier League with just 17 points! They'd only just survived the season before, but they weren't able to repeat the feat in 2015-16, which included a pretty miserable 11-game losing streak!

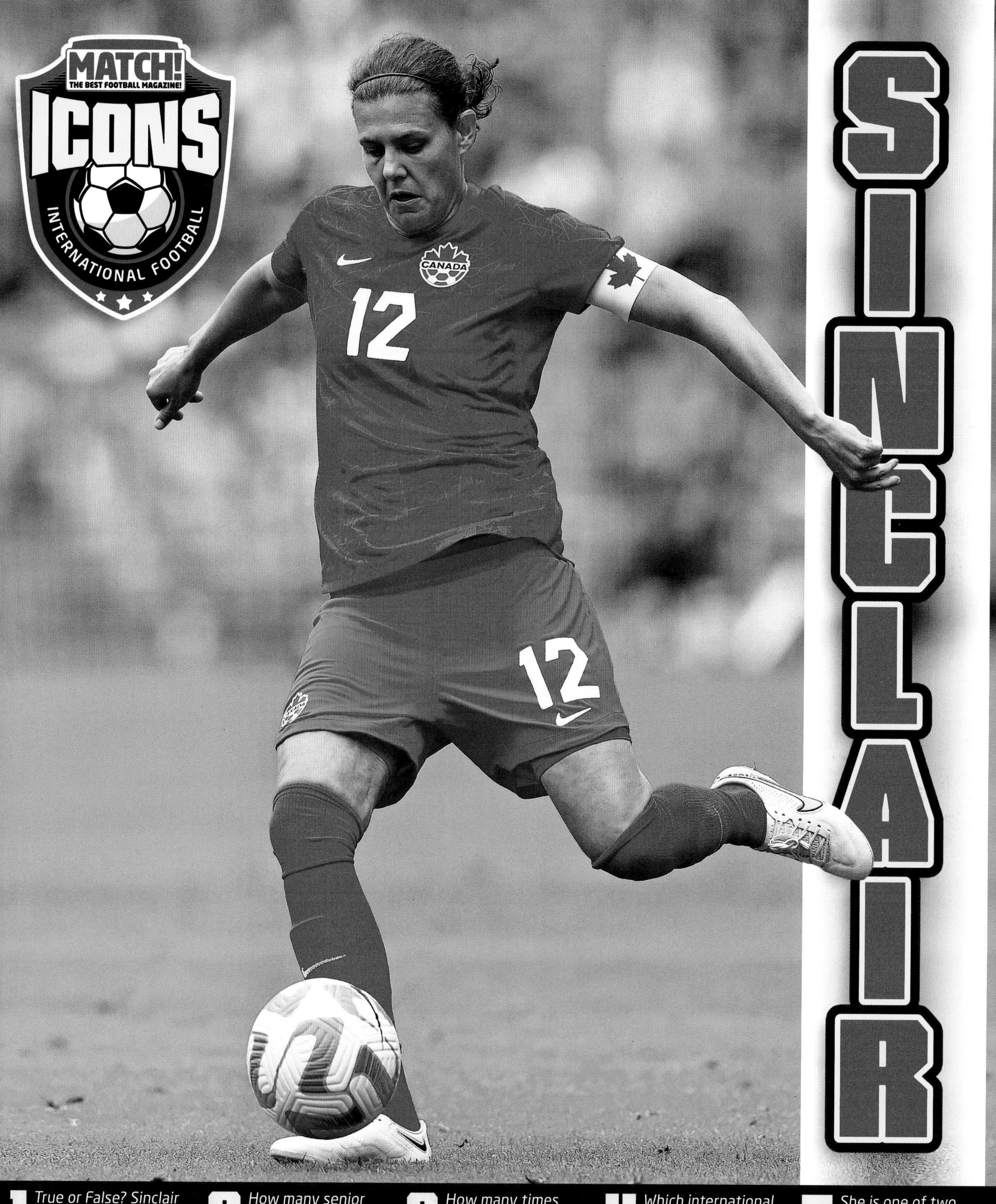

1 True or False? Sinclair is the world's all-time leading goalscorer for both men and women's international sides!

2 How many senior international caps did she win for Canada between 2000 and 2023 – more or less than 300?

3 How many times was the lethal forward named Canada Soccer Player of the Year – five, 11 or 14?

4 Which international trophy did Christine never lift during her wicked career – the World Cup or the Olympics?

5 She is one of two women's players to score at five World Cup tournaments. Can you name the other?

ANSWERS ON PAGE 94

PACKED EVERY ISSUE WITH...

MASSIVE STARS

RED-HOT GEAR

EPIC FEATURES

AMAZING POSTERS

CARTOONS & QUIZZES

SUBSCRIBE TO MATCH!...

CALL
01959 543 747
QUOTE: MATAN25

ONLINE
SHOP.KELSEY.CO.UK/MATAN25

Terms & Conditions: Discounted subscription offer may not include all covermount gifts that are included with retail copies. UK Direct Debit offer only. Offer ends December 31, 2025. *Discounts are calculated on the full cover price, plus Kelsey Media's standard postage and packing price. Overseas and UK debit/credit card offers, as well as digital subscription offers, are available at shop.kelsey.co.uk/MATCH. Your subscription will start with the next available issue and you will receive 26 issues in a year. You will pay £39.99 for 13 issues via Direct Debit. Calls charged at your standard network rate. Lines open Monday-Friday, 8:30am-5:30pm. Full terms and conditions can be found at shop.kelsey.co.uk/terms. Data Protection: We take great care in handling your personal details and these will only ever be used as set out in our privacy policy, which can be viewed at shop.kelsey.co.uk/privacy-policy. You may unsubscribe at any time. If you decide to cancel your subscription, we will put a stop to any further payments being taken and will send the remaining issues that you have already paid for.

QUIZ ANSWERS!

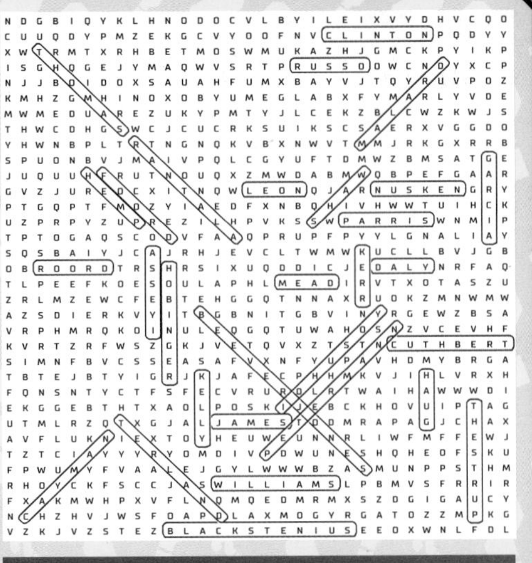

Premier League Quiz — Pages 24-25

Who Started Where?: 1C; 2A; 3E; 4B; 5F; 6D.

Job Swap: Harry Toffolo.

Legendary: 1. Everton; 2. Chelsea; 3. Bolton; 4. Middlesbrough; 5. Man. United; 6. Liverpool.

Flag Finder: West Ham.

Footy MisMATCH: See above.

Euro Leagues Quiz — Pages 34-35

Name The Team: 1. Marc-Andre ter Stegen; 2. Jules Kounde; 3. Andreas Christensen; 4. Ronald Araujo; 5. Inigo Martinez; 6. Joao Cancelo; 7. Pedri; 8. Lamine Yamal; 9. Ilkay Gundogan; 10. Frenkie de Jong.

Name The Year: 2016.

MATCH Winner: Vinicius Junior.

Five-A-Side: 1. Brice Samba; 2. Daley Blind; 3. Florian Wirtz; 4. Eduardo Camavinga; 5. Luuk de Jong.

Face In The Crowd: See below.

EFL Quiz — Pages 52-53

Portsmouth Quiz: 1. False; 2. Higher than 20,000; 3. Southampton; 4. Harry Redknapp; 5. Cardiff; 6. Rio Ferdinand.

MATCH Maths: 4 + 24 - 9 = 19.

Face To Face: Dael Fry & Paddy McNair.

Name The Club: Bristol City.

Wordfit: See right.

Women's Footy Quiz — Pages 66-67

Flip For It: 1. Lauren James; 2. Japan; 3. Karoline Olesen; 4. Liverpool; 5. Man. City; 6. adidas.

Stat Attack: Beth Mead.

List It: Your score out of ten.

Odd One Out: Guro Reiten.

Wordsearch: See above.

Quiz Posters

Rooney Quiz: 1. True; 2. 17 years old; 3. Four times; 4. Bobby Charlton; 5. USA.

Henry Quiz: 1. True; 2. Italy; 3. Michel Platini; 4. Olivier Giroud; 5. More than 100.

Alonso Quiz: 1. True; 2. Bayern Munich; 3. France; 4. Xavi; 5. 16 goals.

Rapinoe Quiz: 1. True; 2. Wembley; 3. 34 years old; 4. Golden Ball; 5. Nike.

Sinclair Quiz: 1. True; 2. More than 300; 3. 14 times; 4. World Cup; 5. Marta.

One point for each correct answer!

MY SCORE /156